Doing Case Study Research

Doing Case Study Research

A Practical Guide for Beginning Researchers

Dawson R. Hancock
Bob Algozzine

Teachers College
Columbia University
New York and London

Published by Teachers College Press, 1234 Amsterdam Avenue, New York, NY 10027

Library of Congress Cataloging-in-Publication Data

Hancock, Dawson R.
  Doing case study research : a practical guide for beginning researchers / Dawson R. Hancock, Bob Algozzine.
     p. cm.
  Includes bibliographical references and index.
  ISBN-13: 978-0-8077-4708-7 (cloth : alk. paper)
  ISBN-13: 978-0-8077-4707-0 (pbk. : alk. paper)
  ISBN-10: 0-8077-4708-4 (cloth : alk. paper)
  ISBN-10: 0-8077-4707-6 (pbk : alk. paper)
  1. Education—Research—Methodology. 2. Education—Research—Case studies.
  3. Case method. I. Algozzine, Robert. II. Title.
  LB1028.H313 2006
  370.7'2—dc22
                                                                    2006040499

ISBN-13:   ISBN-10:
978-0-8077-4707-0 (paper) 0-8077-4707-6 (paper)
978-0-8077-4708-7 (cloth) 0-8077-4708-4 (cloth)

Printed on acid-free paper

Manufactured in the United States of America

  13 12 11 10 09 08 07 06   8 7 6 5 4 3 2 1

Contents

Part III:
Putting It All Together

Preface

As university professors teaching quantitative and qualitative methods courses to beginning and advanced graduate students in education and health professions, we are constantly faced with the need for resources that guide novice researchers through the stages of planning and implementing studies. This handbook is a guide for doing case study research. The emphasis throughout is on learning how to plan, conduct, and write up a case study research project. Our goal is to provide sufficient structure, detail, and guidance for beginning researchers to get a handle on what it takes to complete a systematic case study.

Doing Case Study Research begins with an examination of the scientific method (Chapter 1, Scientific Inquiry) as the context for exploring topologies and procedures used to conduct educational research (Chapter 2, Qualitative and Quantitative Research). The rationale and circumstances for conducting a certain type of research, the case study (Chapter 3, Setting the Stage), are followed by a discussion of how to identify literature that informs the research effort (Chapter 4, Determining What We Know). We then describe how to determine an appropriate research design (Chapter 5, Selecting a Design) and how to conduct informative interviews (Chapter 6, Gathering Information from Interviews), observations (Chapter 7, Gathering Information from Observations), and document analyses (Chapter 8, Gathering Information from Documents). After describing how data are acquired, we discuss how to derive meaning from them (Chapter 9, Interpreting the Information) and how to communicate results (Chapter 10, Reporting Findings). Finally, we describe ways to verify, substantiate, and back up the results attained through a case study research effort (Chapter 11, Confirming Findings). Applying the steps examined in this handbook, researchers at all levels will be able to design and conduct a high-quality case study research project.

To facilitate understanding, *Doing Case Study Research* contains many examples that illustrate key concepts contained in the chapters. Sources of additional case study research information are cited throughout the book for those interested in more in-depth information. Finally, each chapter

ends with questions, illustrations, and activities to help prospective researchers apply information that was presented.

KEY FEATURES

Most of the information available about case study research seems to be
written for people who already know a lot about qualitative and quantitative methods. Even books focused specifically on case study research
leave new researchers wondering how to do it. In this brief handbook, we
describe methods that speak directly to beginning investigators and address their needs in a step-by-step approach in the following ways:

- *Doing Case Study Research* is written in language that is accessible to
  individuals who do not have an extensive background in research
  methods; the intended audience is beginning researchers.
- We emphasize learning how to do case study research. From the
  first step of deciding whether a case study is the way to go to the
  last step of verifying and confirming findings before disseminating
  them, this is a very practical, easy-to-read handbook.
- We include plenty of examples from published works as illustrations of each step in doing case study research.
- We end each part of the book with questions and activities designed
  to reinforce what has been learned.
- We include an extensive reference list for use in extending what is
  being taught and as evidence that what we are saying is grounded
  in the body of knowledge that exists about doing case study research.
- We frame the book as a guide for doing case study research; students and advisors can use the book to shape a thesis, dissertation,
  or independent project from conceptualization to completion.

RATIONALE

As part of their academic curriculum, students pursuing baccalaureate,
master's, and doctoral degrees are often required to conduct a research
project or produce a thesis or dissertation. For many of these students,
this is the only occasion during their personal or professional lives that
they will participate in a research effort. *Doing Case Study Research* is written for these students—students who desire to have a prescriptive, step-
by-step guide for conducting a case study research project. There is a large

and complete library of books (some dated, some classic, and some brand new) on the theory and practice of qualitative research (see Creswell, 1998; Ely, Anzul, Friedman, Garner, & Steinmetz, 1991; Erlandson, Harris, Skipper, & Allen, 1993; Flinders & Mills, 1993; Glesne & Peshkin, 1992; Hatch, 2002; Lancy, 1993; Lincoln & Guba, 1985; Mason, 2002; Merriam, 2001; Miles & Huberman, 1994; Patton, 1980, 1990); most of these works address case study research in a very cursory manner. There is a small collection of practical books about selected aspects of case study research. For example, Galvan's (1999) *Writing Literature Reviews* and Seidman's (2006) *Interviewing as Qualitative Research* focus on important aspects of doing research, but do not address the overall process of doing case study research. There are also a few books about case study research (Merriam, 2001; Stake, 1995; Yin, 1994, 2003), but they address more theory than practice and most do not deal successfully with boiling down the essentials of doing case study research for novice investigators. Since the content of these books does not overlap significantly with the information in *Doing Case Study Research*, it would be an excellent companion for any of them. Whereas other books provide important information regarding various approaches to qualitative and case study research, *Doing Case Study Research* synthesizes the information contained in these approaches into a succinct "how-to" guide that systematically illustrates the complete case study research process.

COURSE APPLICATIONS

Doing Case Study Research has a place in any introduction to research or research methods course. It is written primarily for graduate students and others new to doing independent research. We have tried to write it using the same language we use when teaching the content in educational research courses and when we work with master's and doctoral-degree students doing independent research for a thesis or dissertation. Case study research is a complex process. This book is not "case study research for dummies." However, it is also not a complex textbook addressing theories and concepts of doing qualitative research. It is a straightforward attempt to introduce new researchers to the science of doing case study research without overwhelming them by it. It is an attempt to bridge the gap between very brief treatments of case study research typically found in introductory research-methods books and the more general introductions presented in the growing library of qualitative research textbooks. While the book is intended for students likely to engage in thesis or dissertation research as a new experience, *Doing Case Study Research* also has value for advanced undergraduate students doing "senior projects" or other forms of systematic investigation in the social, medical, or behavioral sciences.

We designed the book as a primary resource for students, but another audience is the large number of professors who serve on and sometimes chair thesis and dissertation committees. Often these individuals have little or no formal preparation and no direct experience doing case study research and they are constantly searching for simple, direct resources that offer guidance in their efforts to support their students in matters related to independent research, especially that of a qualitative nature. Because the book provides a step-by-step approach, it is an excellent place for a student and his or her advisor to begin doing case study research together.

Acknowledgments

No one writes a book alone. We would like to thank everyone who has helped us understand qualitative research and case studies over the years. In particular, we owe a special debt to Robert Yin, for a first enthusiastic and interesting exposure more than 20 years ago, and, more recently, to our graduate students Shawnee Wakeman and Bryan Setser, who continually helped us "keep it real." The work was collaborative in the fullest extent and speaks for both of us.

DRH

BA

PART I

Background Information

CHAPTER 1

Scientific Inquiry

Each day we ask questions, large and small, of ourselves and others. A zoologist may ask, "How does a caterpillar evolve into a butterfly?" An educator may ask, "Why does this student behave as he does?" An economist may ask, "What factors shape our society's economic well-being?" A voter may ask, "Who is best qualified to serve as our next president?" Although the types and scope of our questions are limitless, the questions are united by one characteristic—a desire to find an answer. As humans, we are driven to know why things are as they are. When confronted with a novel or perplexing situation, our natural tendency is to ask a question: Who? What? When? Where? Why?

Therefore, in a sense, *all of us are researchers*. Why? Because at its core, research is about answering questions as we attempt to understand the world around us! When you set about the task of finding answers to everyday questions, you are conducting research. Formal research, like that being done for a thesis, a dissertation, or a funded or unfunded project, involves systematic actions that help the researcher add credibility to the questions and answers engaged in his or her research. It involves finding patterns or irregularities in data, which in turn become tentative answers to questions that often form the basis for additional study. Sometimes, answering questions is not as easy as it looks, for several reasons.

First, as humans, we sometimes observe things in different ways or incorrectly. People observing the same event often relate the details of the event very differently, reaching different conclusions about the causes of the event. Second, we often oversimplify things around us. In an attempt to understand a phenomenon, we often reduce it to its essential elements, thereby missing rich details that characterize the true nature of the phenomenon. Third, we sometimes fail to recognize or account for variables that are influencing a situation under investigation. For example, while concluding that a student's poor academic performance results from her laziness, we may fail to realize that the student has a learning disability or a disruptive home life that negatively influences her classroom performance.

To do a better job of answering important questions, we often apply research procedures that allow us to reach conclusions that are sensible, credible, and interpretable.

Research involves determining:

1. what we want to study (the research question)
2. how do we want to study it (the design)
3. whom we want to study (the "case," "cases," or "sample")
4. how best to acquire information (the data-collection techniques)
5. how best to analyze or interpret the information that we acquire (the data analysis)
6. how and with whom to share our findings (the dissemination process)
7. how to confirm our findings (the verification process).

To accomplish these tasks, researchers have devised a number of organizing frameworks.

Think of an organizing framework as a road map. A road map establishes for a traveler the possibilities for getting from one location to another. Although a map does not specify the exact route to follow, would you ever attempt to drive across the country without a map? Probably not! In the same sense, a researcher should not conduct a research project without an organizing framework. This framework establishes for the researcher the defining features and possibilities for acquiring answers to a research question. Just as a map allows a traveler to make critical decisions regarding his route, an organizing framework allows a researcher to make important decisions that may greatly impact the nature of the research study. Therefore, before conducting a research study, a researcher must be familiar with the most significant organizing frameworks.

Most organizing frameworks are labeled by their essential attributes. Although the various frameworks are not mutually exclusive, each one possesses its own fundamental characteristics. One common organizing framework, concerned with the generalization of research findings, is the distinction between *descriptive* and *inferential* research. In descriptive studies, information is collected for the purpose of describing a specific group with no intention of going beyond that group. In inferential studies, researchers desire to go beyond a specific group in order to make generalized statements about a larger population. For example, a medical doctor studying the behaviors of several medical interns to determine how they behave in a particular hospital would engage in a descriptive study. However, if the doctor's intent was to select and study interns who were representative of a general population of interns in order to generalize her findings to that general population, she would conduct an inferential study.

Another organizing framework involves the level of research experimentation. True *experimental* research is characterized by manipulation of an independent variable combined with random assignment of participants to groups. An example might be a physiologist interested in the impact of exercise on students' academic performance. Comparing the academic performance of 30 students randomly assigned to an exercise class to that of a group of students not in the class would help establish whether the exercise class influenced the students' academic performance. An alternative to true experimental designs are quasi-experimental designs in which variables are manipulated but no random assignment of participants occurs. Finally, nonexperimental designs involve no variable manipulation and no random assignment. These three designs range in their ability to identify cause-and-effect relationships from very good (true experimental) to poor (nonexperimental).

The distinction between *basic* and *applied* research represents another organizing framework. Basic research involves the examination of variables in order to construct or verify a theory (i.e., an explanation of a particular phenomenon). By contrast, applied research is concerned primarily with addressing an existing problem or issue. Hence, basic research is sometimes called theory-based research, whereas applied research is sometimes called problem-based research. Although the thrust of these two approaches differ, in reality they overlap in that practical outcomes often result from basic research while contributions to a theory often result from an applied-research effort. For example, a researcher may engage in a basic-research study intended primarily to substantiate Bloom's (1984) theory of mastery learning—a theory designed to explain how all children can achieve their full academic potential. In doing this, he may also be conducting applied research by helping a school district understand how its children may be taught to perform better academically.

A final organizing framework classifies research as *quantitative* or *qualitative*. Although many research studies apply characteristics of both approaches, the principles and activities inherent in these two approaches allow researchers to plan and conduct their research in very different ways. Most fundamentally, quantitative researchers use numbers, normally in the form of statistics, to explain phenomena. Qualitative researchers, however, use words to describe trends or patterns in research settings. Because these descriptions greatly oversimplify the approaches' distinctions and because almost all research can be classified using the characteristics of these approaches, we have devoted the following chapter of this book to their full explanation and to how case study research fits within the qualitative more than within the quantitative framework.

CONTENT REVIEW

1. Why are all of us *researchers*?
2. Why should a researcher use an organizing framework to plan and conduct her study?
3. What are some of the most common organizing frameworks used by researchers?

ACTIVITIES AND APPLICATIONS FOR
PROSPECTIVE RESEARCHERS

1. Think of a time when you and someone else observed the same situation but interpreted it differently or attributed the cause of the situation to different factors. Based on the information in this chapter, why might those differences have occurred?
2. Think of three situations in your life during the past week in which you wanted to know *why* something occurred as it did. Which organizing framework(s) of scientific inquiry might you use to develop an explanation for each situation?
3. Think of a topic that you may want to explore as a case study research project. What observations have you made related to this topic? Which organizing framework may be applicable to your research study?

CHAPTER 2

Qualitative and Quantitative Research

A particularly useful organizing framework for beginning researchers involves understanding the differences between qualitative and quantitative research. The distinctions between these approaches are numerous. Selection of the approach to use in a specific research effort depends largely on the goals and preferences of the researcher. To help you understand the approaches, consider the following example.

Assume that students at a particular university are disenchanted with the university's policies and practices. Student complaints are common, attrition is high, and morale is low. The university's president decides to research possible causes of this situation. In doing so, the president may decide to follow a more qualitative or quantitative research approach. Using a qualitative approach, the president would use information collected from interviews with specific disenchanted students or other sources to develop an explanation for the problem. Using a quantitative approach, the president might review statistics from other universities or gather and compare numbers reflective of reasons for leaving school from different groups of students (e.g., some planning to leave and some planning to stay). A number of factors might influence the president's decision about which approach to follow.

If time and resources are limited, a quantitative approach may be more appropriate. This is because quantitative research often involves instruments, such as surveys and tests, to measure specific variables, such as the students' source of disenchantment, from large groups of people. These instruments typically produce useful data in short time periods with reasonable investment of personnel and materials. In contrast, a qualitative approach may require individual interviews, focus groups, observations, a review of existing documents, or a number of these. Although these data sources would result in a wealth of rich information, considerable time and resources may be required to adequately represent the area being studied.

If little is known about an issue, a qualitative approach might be more useful. Whereas a typical quantitative research project identifies and investigates the impact of only a few variables, qualitative research attempts to explore a host of factors that may be influencing a situation. Therefore, if the university president has not yet discovered specific possible causes of the students' unhappiness, he may wish to use the more holistic qualitative approach to investigate an array of possible sources of the problem that could later serve as the basis for a comparative quantitative study.

If access to people who can participate in the research study is limited, a quantitative approach may be preferred. This is because quantitative research can often be accomplished with minimal involvement of participants. In contrast, the individual interviews and focus groups inherent in qualitative research may slow one's research efforts if access to individuals is difficult. For example, a university president may have difficulty finding students for his study if their schedules preclude participation.

If the consumers of research findings prefer words to numbers, a qualitative approach may be best. For example, disenchanted university students may prefer the richly elaborated explanations of their concerns that are more normally produced by qualitative studies than by quantitative approaches. A university's governing board, however, may be more receptive to findings derived from quantifiable data than to results based on words, feelings, and expressions.

Another factor affecting decisions to use a qualitative or quantitative approach involves the relationship of the researcher to those being studied. In qualitative research, the goal is to understand the situation under investigation primarily from the participants' and not the researcher's perspective. This is called the *emic*, or insider's, perspective, as opposed to the *etic*, or outsider's, perspective. A university president may learn more by examining potential sources of student disenchantment through the eyes of the students than through his own.

Finally, because the researcher is the primary instrument for data collection and analysis in qualitative research, she must spend significant amounts of time in the environment of those being studied. In contrast, a quantitative researcher often seeks to remain *blind* to the experimental conditions of her research in order to maintain objectivity and to avoid influencing the variables under investigation. Therefore, a university president interested in qualitative research must be willing and able to devote considerable amounts of time to interactions with students, whereas a quantitatively oriented university president can expect to spend less time with students.

Clearly, qualitative and quantitative approaches to research differ in many ways, each with its own unique features. Neither approach is right or wrong, although one approach may be more appropriate than the other depending on the nature of the research question and predisposition of the researcher. In some cases, researchers implement activities of both approaches in the same research study.

Although the general characteristics of qualitative research are the same, differences exist between specific types of qualitative research. What are the types of qualitative research and how do they differ? Many types have evolved from various disciplines, such as anthropology, sociology, psychology, history, biology, and education. For illustrative purposes, we highlight five major types (Creswell, 1998), paying special attention to case studies—a type of qualitative research used in many disciplines.

Phenomenological studies are one type of qualitative research. These studies explore the meaning of several people's lived experiences around a specific issue or phenomenon. The assumption is that there is an essence or central meaning of an experience shared by individuals that can be investigated and explained through research. In phenomenological studies, the experiences of different people are analyzed to describe the essence of a phenomenon, such as the essence of having cancer or of being a minority in a majority setting.

Ethnographic studies, a second type of qualitative research, investigate intact cultural or social groups to find and describe beliefs, values, and attitudes that structure the behavior, language, and interactions of the group. Findings are based primarily on observations by the researcher, who is immersed in the group's setting for an extended period of time. The researcher observes and records group members' voices with the goal of creating a cultural portrait.

In *grounded-theory qualitative research*, a researcher seeks to create a theory that explains some action, interaction, or process. The investigator is the primary instrument of data collection and attempts to inductively derive meaning from the data. The product of this type of qualitative research is a substantive theory that is "grounded" in the data. Substantive theories tend to explain more specific, everyday situations than do more formal, all-encompassing theories.

Biographical studies, including life and oral histories and classical and interpretive biographies, constitute another type of qualitative research in which a researcher explores a single individual and her or his experiences. Findings are derived largely from oral story-telling by the person being studied or from documents and archival materials related to the person's life. The goal is to find and present themes that indicate important points in the person's life that truly reveal the individual.

Case studies represent another type of qualitative research. They are different from other types in that they are intensive analyses and descriptions

Table 2.1. Comparison of General Research Traditions

Quantitative Studies	*Qualitative Studies*	*Case Studies*
Researcher identifies topic or question(s) of interest and selects participants and arranges procedures that provide answers that are accepted with predetermined degree of confidence; research questions are often stated in hypotheses that are accepted or rejected using statistical tests and analyses.	Researcher identifies topic or question(s) of interest; collects information from a variety of sources, often as a participant observer; and accepts the analytical task as one of discovering answers that emerge from information that is available as a result of the study.	Research identifies topic or question(s) of interest, determines appropriate unit to represent it, and defines what is known based on careful analysis of multiple sources of information about the "case."
Research process may vary greatly from context being investigated (e.g., survey of how principals spend their time) or appropriately reflect it (e.g., observation of how principals spend their time).	Research process is designed to reflect, as much as possible, the natural, ongoing context being investigated; information is often gathered by participant observers (individuals actively engaged, immersed, or involved in the information collection setting or activity).	Research process is defined by systematic series of steps designed to provide careful analysis of the case.
Information collection may last a few hours or a few days, but generally is of short-term duration using carefully constructed measures designed specifically to generate valid and reliable information under the conditions of the study.	Information collection may last a few months or as long as it takes for an adequate answer to emerge; the time frame for the study is often not defined at the time the research is undertaken.	Information collection may last a few hours, a few days, a few months, or as long as is necessary to adequately "define" the case.
Report of the outcomes of the process is generally expository, consisting of a series of statistical answers to questions under investigation.	Report of outcomes of the process is generally narrative, consisting of a series of "pages to the story" or "chapters to the book."	Report of outcomes of the process is generally narrative in nature, consisting of a series of illustrative descriptions of key aspects of the case.

of a single unit or system bounded by space and time. Topics often examined in case studies include individuals, events, or groups. Through case studies, researchers hope to gain in-depth understanding of situations and meaning for those involved. Merriam (2001) suggests that insights gleaned from case studies can directly influence policy, procedures, and future research.

Although case studies are discussed extensively in the literature and employed frequently in practice, little has been written regarding the specific steps one may use to successfully plan, conduct, and share the results of a case study project. The following part of this book fills that void.

ILLUSTRATIONS FROM PRACTICE

Both quantitative and qualitative methods, including case studies, have strong traditions within social and behavioral science research. In fact, each has been used to address important research questions and advance theory and knowledge in many different disciplines. Each method begins with identification of questions to be answered (based on what is already known) and ends with a documentation of answers grounded in systematic analysis of information gathered using appropriate methods. (See Table 2.1 for a comparison of the general research traditions associated with each research method.)

CONTENT REVIEW

1. What are some major differences between qualitative and quantitative research?
2. Under what circumstances might you elect to engage in qualitative or quantitative research?
3. What are some of the major types of qualitative research?

ACTIVITIES AND APPLICATIONS FOR PROSPECTIVE RESEARCHERS

1. Think of a situation or event about which you might decide to use a quantitative research approach. Think of a different situation or event in which you might want to employ qualitative research. Why would you use one approach rather than the other?

2. What are examples of some studies reflective of each of the five types of qualitative research discussed in this chapter?
3. How might the research topic that you identified in Chapter 1 lend itself to examination through qualitative research? Which type of qualitative research might be most applicable?

PART II

Stages of Doing
Case Study Research

CHAPTER 3

Setting the Stage

Many people think of case studies as clinical descriptions of people with unique characteristics or symptoms and of treatments used to help them. Case study research represents a much broader view. It means conducting an empirical investigation of a contemporary phenomenon within its natural context using multiple sources of evidence (Yin, 2003). The topics of case study research vary widely. For example, case studies of programs, events, persons, processes, institutions, social groups, and other contemporary phenomena have been completed. Sometimes people use the term *case study* as a catchall category for research that is not a survey, an observational study, or an experiment and is not statistical in nature (Merriam, 2001). In fact, researchers from many disciplines and many paradigms (qualitative and quantitative) call their work case studies, and they generally agree on several important characteristics that define case study research (Hatch, 2002, p. 30).

First, although case study research sometimes focuses on an individual representative of a group (e.g., a female principal), more often it addresses a phenomenon (e.g., a particular event, situation, program, or activity). For example, a school administrator might want to learn about what happens in his district during a transition from traditional to block scheduling (*event*), a classroom teacher may want to explore factors that influence student attrition at her school (*situation*), a nurse may desire to learn more about employment practices at his hospital (*program*), or a technology specialist may seek greater insights into decision making processes that influence the adoption of software programs in his organization (*activity*). These phenomena represent the focus of most case studies but are not mutually exclusive.

Second, the phenomenon being researched is studied in its natural context, bounded by space and time. The administrator's investigation of block scheduling occurs in a specific school system during a specific time period. The teacher's study of factors influencing student attrition is grounded in her particular school during a particular academic year. The nurse will examine employment practices only in his hospital and for a specific period of time. The technology specialist will restrict his investigation of software adoption procedures to his own organization's practices since the purchase of a computer mainframe. Clearly, context is important in case study research, and its benefits are a strength of doing intensive investigations of individuals or groups as well as events, situations, programs, activities, and other phenomena of interest.

Third, case study research is richly descriptive, because it is grounded in deep and varied sources of information. It employs quotes of key participants, anecdotes, prose composed from interviews, and other literary techniques to create mental images that bring to life the complexity of the many variables inherent in the phenomenon being studied. For example, the administrator illustrates the transition from traditional to block scheduling with school attendance records, focus group interviews, surveys, and end-of-grade achievement scores. A high school teacher presents statements from her students and their parents to illustrate why some people drop out of school. In her case study, the nurse includes a brief narrative story that exemplifies typical employment procedures at her hospital. The technology specialist cites examples of existing practices that influence organizational decision-making regarding the adoption of software packages. Hence, information is explored and mined in the case study environment for a more thorough examination of the given phenomenon.

Additional similarities and differences sometimes found in other forms of research also characterize case study research. For example, in contrast with experimental research, case study research is generally more exploratory than confirmatory; that is, the case study researcher normally seeks to identify themes or categories of behavior and events rather than prove relationships or test hypotheses. Because it involves collecting and analyzing information from multiple sources, such as interviews, observations, and existing documents, case study research sometimes requires the researcher to spend more time in the environment being investigated than is the case with other types of research. Finally, as with most research, doing case studies creates opportunities for the researcher to explore additional questions by the act of investigating a topic in detail.

Doing case study research means identifying a topic that lends itself to in-depth analysis in a natural context using multiple sources of information. Once the stage has been set, we must determine what is known and not known about the topic to create an important research question.

WHAT HAS BEEN STUDIED USING CASE STUDY RESEARCH?

The topics of case study research vary widely, just like the topics of any other type of research. For example, an event that occurred on campus or a situation that has particular relevance for a researcher would be appropriate areas for case studies. Case study researchers also study programs or activities that are of special interest. The following examples illustrate some events, situations, programs, and activities that have been studied with case study research.

Events

Asmussen, K. J., & Creswell, J. W. (1995). Campus response to a student gunman. *Journal of Higher Education, 66*(5), 575–591.

This case study describes a campus response to a gunman incident in which a student attempted to fire a gun at his classmates. The study provides a detailed description of the gunman incident; a chronology of the first 2 weeks of events following the incident; and details about the city, the campus, and the building in which the incident occurred. Findings resulting from data collection through multiple sources of information, such as interviews, observations, documents, and audiovisual materials, are presented. From the data analysis, denial, fear, safety, retriggering, and campus planning emerge as prominent concerns. These themes are combined into two overarching perspectives, an organizational and a psychological or social-psychological response, providing "layers" of analysis in the study and broader interpretations of the meaning of the case. The authors suggest that campuses plan their responses to campus violence and advance key questions to be addressed when preparing these plans.

Benton-Kupper, J. (1999). Teaching in the block: Perceptions from within. *High School Journal, 83*(1), 26–35.

Alternative scheduling, also referred to as block scheduling, is gaining more attention as educational systems explore various methods of how time is used. The purpose of this case study was to explore the experiences of three high school English teachers in their 2nd year of transition from a traditional seven-period day schedule (45-minute periods) to a block four-period day schedule (87-minute periods). Data were gathered from the three teachers through interviews, observations, and collection of documents. Data analysis involved reviewing, coding, categorizing, synthesizing, and interpreting the information attained from the data sources. The analysis produced themes (variety of instructional strategies and depth of content taught) both within each individual's situation as well as across the individuals' situations. Findings suggest that block schedules provide opportunities for instructional strategies that actively engage the student in learning and that the altered time format lets teachers provide more in-depth coverage of content as a result of additional materials, discussions, and projects. The results of this study have implications for curriculum, instruction, and staff development related to block scheduling.

Stine, D. E. (1998). *A change in administration: A significant organizational life event* (Report No. EA029296). Educational Management. (ERIC Document Reproduction Service No. ED425509).

This case study examines a principal's transition to a middle school in Southern California. Data were collected through interviews of two district-level administrative employees, two site-level administrative employees, one site-level counselor, eight certificated employees, and four classified employees. Information was collected from journal entries, observations, and document analysis of faculty meeting minutes, memoranda to staff, a statement of mutual expectations and educational leadership, and a strategic plan. The study describes the principal's background, conditions under which he assumed the principalship, and philosophy of dialogue. It highlights how he took control, the steps that went into formulating the action plan for the school, and statements from staff members regarding the school's transformation. The findings suggest that the transition process involved five major stages: (1) taking hold, (2) immersion, (3) reshaping, (4) consolidation, and (5) refinement. Success was associated with (1) assessing the organization and diagnosing its problems, (2) building a management team focused on a set of shared expectations, and (3) bringing about timely changes that addressed organizational problems.

Situations

Hughes, M. (1998). Turning points in the lives of young inner-city men forgoing destructive criminal behaviors: A qualitative study. *Social Work Research, 22*(3), 143–151.

This case study explored the lives of 20 inner-city African American and Latino American young men previously involved in trajectories of destructive behavior, including violence, illegal drug marketing, and other crimes, who made positive behavioral changes and are now contributing to their community's well-being. In-depth interviews with the men were used to examine their life courses from the time of their earliest memories. Personal and environmental transitions that contributed to their decisions to change were uncovered. Factors affecting their transition experiences included maturation, respect and concern for children, fear of physical harm or incarceration, contemplation time, and support and modeling by others. Implications for social service providers, policymakers, and youth program staff are discussed.

Ladany, N., O'Brien, K. M., Hill, C. E., Melincoff, D. S., Knox, S., & Peterson, D. A. (1997). Sexual attraction toward clients, use of supervision, and prior training: A qualitative study of pre-doctoral psychology interns. *Journal of Counseling Psychology, 44*(4), 413–424.

In this case study, interviews were conducted with 13 predoctoral psychology interns about an experience of sexual attraction toward a client, use of supervision to address the sexual attraction, and prior training regarding sexual attraction. Results indicated that sexual attraction to clients consisted of physical and interpersonal aspects. Therapists believed that they were more invested and attentive than usual to clients to whom they were sexually attracted, and therapists indicated that sexual attraction created distance, distraction, and loss of objectivity. In terms of supervision, only half the participants disclosed their sexual attraction to supervisors, and supervisors seldom initiated the discussion. Furthermore, trainees found it helpful when supervisors normalized the sexual attraction and provided the opportunity to explore feelings in supervision. Finally, trainees believed that their training did not adequately address therapist sexual attraction.

Place, A. W., & Wood, G. S. (1999). A case study of traditionally underrepresented individuals' experiences in a doctoral program. *Journal for a Just and Caring Education, 5*(4), 442–456.

This case study was designed to improve understanding of students of color in a university doctoral program. In-depth, semistructured interviews were conducted and recorded on three occasions with 11 doctoral students. The first interview was the least structured interview. The two subsequent interviews during the following year and a half were slightly more structured in order to explore areas in which more than one student identified a related concept. Two researchers worked separately and collaboratively, using inductive analysis to identify themes after repeated examination of the initial interview data. The following themes were determined when both researchers agreed that the data justified their existence: (1) Faculty need to be from and to read works of other cultures; (2) females see gender issues as more important than racial issues when they are separated but object when they are dealt with separately; (3) diversity is multifaceted and should be dealt with as individuals perceive the issue; (4) students often experience apprehension and self-doubt as they enter doctoral programs; (5) as they begin to succeed academically, students experience stronger self-efficacy but do not view the doctorate as their most important source of self-esteem; (6) students believe their presence influences others; and (7) students of color have more similarities than differences with European American peers, but differ in their perceptions of the extent to which the program has a multicultural perspective.

Programs

Bond, L. B., Jaeger, R., Smith, T., & Hattie, J. (2001). Defrocking the National Board: The certification system of the National Board for Professional Teaching Standards. *Education Matters, 1*(2), 79–82.

The case study explored the teacher certification process of the National Board for Professional Teaching Standards (NBPTS). Researchers collected data on 65 NBPTS-certified teachers through observations of the teachers in their classrooms, documents that reflected the teachers' abilities, data collected from questionnaires administered to the teachers and their students, and interviews of the teachers and selected students. The study found that NBPTS-certified teachers outperformed their noncertified counterparts on many measures of good teaching and that students taught by these teachers demonstrated deeper understanding of concepts than did students taught by noncertified teachers. However, the study raises questions regarding whether the NBPTS certification process is a valid and cost-effective way of identifying the nation's best teachers and enhancing student achievement.

D'Emidio-Caston, M., & Brown, J. H. (1998). The other side of the story: Student narratives on the California Drug, Alcohol, and Tobacco Education programs. *Evaluation Review, 22*(1), 95–117.

Within the context of a large-scale, comprehensive evaluation of the California Drug Alcohol Tobacco Education (DATE) program, this case study sought to extend knowledge of student perceptions of preventive education using a naturalistic approach. The constant comparative method was used to analyze 40 focus group interviews of at-risk and thriving groups conducted in 11 high, middle, and elementary school districts. Results suggest that students use "story" to make sense of prevention education and distinguish use from abuse. High school students believe that hearing only one side of the substance use/abuse story and strict expulsion policies alienate students most in need of help. Implications for the use of story as an assessment tool are discussed, as are implications for substance use prevention policy.

Howe, K., Eisenhart, M., & Betebenner, D. (2002). The price of public school choice. *Educational Leadership, 59*(7), 20–25.

This case study investigated the impact of the school choice programs in Boulder Valley School District. Researchers examined records from six school years on open enrollment, test scores, demographics, funding, and fund-raising in 55 of the district's 57 schools. In addition, to collect data about attitudes toward school choice, researchers conducted surveys of principals by telephone and then held focus group discussions and conducted written surveys with parents and selected educators. The principals, parents, and educators totaled 466 individuals representing 43 schools. To ascertain the attitudes of parents who had not participated in open enrollment and were not active in the schools, researchers called potential respondents selected at random from eight geographical regions until 30 completed surveys were obtained from each region. A synthesis of all data suggested that the school choice programs had resulted in increased stratification of schools according to race, ethnicity, income, resources, and achievement.

Activities

Horn, E., Lieber, J., Li, S., Sandall, S., & Schwartz, I. (2000). Supporting young children's IEP goals in inclusive settings through embedded learning opportunities. *Topics in Early Childhood Education, 20*(4), 208–224.

This study presents three cases designed to assess the feasibility of teachers in inclusive early education programs supporting young people's learning objectives through embedded learning opportunities (ELO). The studies were conducted in three separate inclusive early childhood education programs located in three different states on four children with disabilities and their classroom teachers. The examination of the ELO procedure included assessment of teachers' planning and implementation, the impact on child performance of specific learning objectives, and the teachers' perceptions of the ELO strategy. Researchers attained data through a variety of collection techniques, including direct observation using strict protocols and interviews of teachers. The results revealed that all teachers demonstrated increases in use of instructional behaviors toward targeted objectives, and the children showed concomitant increases in performance of targeted objectives. However, clear differences between teachers existed regarding the consistency and frequency of implementation of the instructional support strategies.

Mueller, A., & Fleming, T. (2001). Cooperative learning: Listening to how children work at school. *Journal of Educational Research*, *94*(5), 259–366.

Cooperative and collaborative learning are recognized as valuable components of classroom learning. However, many questions remain regarding how teachers might structure and guide children's group-learning experiences. This ethnographic case study examined 29 Grade 6 and Grade 7 students who worked in groups over 5 weeks. Data included audiotape recordings of six groups of children working together across 11 work sessions, student interviews, children's self-evaluations and drawings, and research reports. Findings revealed that when working in groups, children require periods of unstructured time to organize themselves and to learn how to work together toward a mutual goal. In addition, researchers found that children in an autocratically led group seemed discontented, often aggressive, and lacking in initiative. Youngsters in groups without a leader experienced similar problems: members appeared frustrated and much of the work remained unfinished. In marked contrast, children in groups organized with a democratic leader—someone who allowed the group to set its own agendas and priorities—appeared far more productive and socially satisfied and demonstrated greater originality and independence in the work they completed.

Rhoads, R. A. (1998). In the service of citizenship: A study of student involvement in community service. *The Journal of Higher Education*, *69*(3), 277–297.

This case study examines social responsibility among higher-education students, focusing on the role of education as source of citizenship preparation. Founded on John Dewey's philosophical work and using methodological strategies associated with naturalistic inquiry, data were collected using a variety of techniques, including formal and informal interviews, surveys, participant observation, and document analysis. During the 6-year period in which data were collected, 108 students participated in interviews, 66 students completed open-ended surveys, and more than 200 students were observed. Once collected, the data were read repeatedly in an effort to identify important and relevant themes. Students' exploration of self, understanding of others, and views of social good are key themes explored in this study.

ILLUSTRATIONS FROM PRACTICE

Questions reflective of how data are collected and procedures that are commonly used when conducting a case study are presented in Tables 3.1 and 3.2. Creswell (1998, 2002) presents additional information on similarities and differences in data collection activities and other procedures related to doing research across approaches.

Table 3.1. Case Study Characteristics and Data Collection Questions

Characteristic	Data Collection Question
A bound "case," such as a process, activity, event, program, or multiple individuals, is investigated.	What is studied? (Define the case.)
A gatekeeper provides access to information and assistance in gaining confidence of participants.	What are any concerns related to access and rapport? (Establish access and rapport.)
A "case" or "cases," an "atypical" case, or a "maximum variation" or "extreme" case is defined.	What sites or individuals are going to be studied? (Sample with purpose.)
A collection of forms, such as documents and records, interviews, observations, or physical artifacts, is compiled.	What type(s) of information will be collected? (Delimit data.)
A variety of approaches (e.g., field notes, interviews, and observations) are used to gather data.	How is information compiled? (Record information.)
Concerns may emerge related to intensive data gathering.	Is data collection difficult? (Address field issues.)
A large amount of data (e.g., field notes, transcriptions, computer databases) is typically collected.	How is information stored? (Store data for analysis.)

Adapted from J. W. Creswell. (1998). *Qualitative inquiry and research design: Choosing among five traditions.* Thousand Oaks, CA: Sage.

Table 3.2. Procedures Commonly Used in Case Studies

Procedure	Case Study
Intent, appropriate design, and how intent relates to research problem are defined.	The problem focuses on developing an in-depth understanding of a "case" or bounded system. It is related to understanding that an event, activity, process, or one or more individuals and the type of "case," such as intrinsic, instrumental, or collective, is delimited.
The plan to receive approval and gain access to study sites and participants is defined.	Approval from institutional review board is obtained. A research site is located using purposeful sampling procedures. Number of cases is determined and gatekeeper to provide access is identified. Provisions for respecting the site are defined.
Data are collected emphasizing time in the field, multiple sources of information, and collaboration.	Extensive information is gathered using multiple forms of data collection (observations, interviews, documents), including audiovisual materials and other relevant sources.
Data are analyzed and interpreted relative to the design.	Data are reviewed to develop an overall understanding. Case(s) is (are) described in detail and a context for the description is delimited. Key issues or themes about the case(s) are developed. A cross-case analysis is conducted if appropriate.
Research report suitable for dissemination is prepared.	Reporting focuses on describing the case with description, analysis, and interpretation addressed differently or equally. Decision is made to emphasize objective or subjective reporting, including biases and generalizations to other cases.

Adapted from J. W. Creswell. (2002). *Educational research: Planning, conducting, and evaluating quantitative and qualitative research.* Upper Saddle River, NJ: Prentice Hall.

CONTENT REVIEW

1. What are some general topics often studied in case study research?
2. What are some characteristics of case study research?
3. What is meant by the phrase *case study research is generally more exploratory than confirmatory*?

ACTIVITIES AND APPLICATIONS FOR
PROSPECTIVE RESEARCHERS

1. Find a journal article (not discussed in this chapter) that describes case study research focused on an event, a situation, a program, or an activity. Why is this article an example of case study research?
2. Find an article that describes case study research and an article that describes a similar topic studied using another type of research. What are three similarities and three differences in how this work was completed?
3. How might the characteristics of case study research may be applicable to your own research project? Which characteristics would you emphasize in your work?

CHAPTER 4

Determining What We Know

Once you identify what you will investigate in your case study research, you should determine what is already known and not known about the topic by reviewing what has been written about it. Your purposes in reviewing the literature are to establish the conceptual foundation for the study, to define and establish the importance of your research question, to identify strengths and weaknesses of models and designs that others have used to study it, and to identify the style and form used by experts to extend the knowledge base surrounding your question.

Examining existing literature helps researchers identify viable and important research questions or hypotheses. For example, an administrator interested in block scheduling should base his work on what others believe about how classes are scheduled and the need for research demonstrating that this innovative practice does or does not make a difference in how high schools educate America's youth. Information on what is known about block scheduling provides a basis for framing case study research on scheduling practices. A classroom teacher interested in identifying factors that influence student attrition may discover a theory suggesting that students sometimes drop out of school when teachers' instructional strategies fail to match the students' preferred learning styles. As a result, when researching her own school, this teacher may want to explore the types of instruction normally employed and how students' achievement is influenced by that instruction. In another situation, a nurse wanting to know more about employment practices may realize through her review of existing literature that discriminatory hiring practices pervade hospitals in her region. As a result, this nurse may elect to focus her initial case study questions on the hiring practices that exist in her own hospital. Finally, a technology specialist examining computer software adoption practices may discover from professional journals that companies often choose software based on its cost and availability more than on its usefulness. With this knowledge, the technology specialist may question his company's decision makers on the specific criteria for selecting software in his organization. Identifying what is known and not known helps you establish the importance of your topic.

Second, reading existing literature helps researchers identify possible research designs and strategies for their own research efforts. For example, the administrator may uncover a report that matches his thoughts and ideas about how to study the use of block scheduling in schools. A teacher may find that previous research efforts successfully employed a case study research design involving psychological constructs to explain why students drop out of school. A nurse may learn from previously conducted studies that employment practices can best be determined by observing the actual behaviors of hospital administrators and not by examining an organization's written employment policies. A technology specialist may discern from previous investigations that examining existing documents is the best way to identify organizational decision-making processes regarding the adoption of software packages. Studying the literature helps you identify the strengths and weaknesses of models and designs that others have used before you. This information is valuable in planning your own research.

Third, reading the works of others helps researchers learn the formats and procedures for writing and communicating their own findings to others. For example, an administrator may find an interview protocol that will meet her needs with a little modification. A teacher may discover that the best information regarding causes of student attrition is found in locally produced and disseminated documents written in language that is comprehensible to non-research-oriented educators. A nurse may determine that the most useful research findings on hospital employment practices are found in professional journals created by national labor unions. As a result of reading material on his topic, a technology specialist may realize that the publications of professional organizations produce the most authoritative information about software selection practices. Identifying what is known and not known helps you learn the style and form used by experts to extend the knowledge base surrounding your topic.

Doing case study research means determining what we know about a research question to establish its importance and the need for further research about it, to identify strengths and weaknesses of previous research, and to identify areas of sufficient and insufficient study as well as methods used to study it. Once you have established the questions and need for your study, you are ready to select a design to guide your research effort.

HOW TO DO A LITERATURE REVIEW

Galvan (1999) provides a straightforward guide for use in writing literature reviews and includes some key "directions."

- Select a topic and identify literature to review:
  - Identify appropriate databases, review articles, and classic
    studies
  - Review recent literature first and work backward
  - Define what is known and what is not known as quickly as
    possible
- Analyze the literature:
  - Use consistent form for summarizing articles
  - Look for strengths and weakness
  - Identify gaps in what is known
- Criticize the literature:
  - Summarize nature of the research (e.g., quantitative/qualita-
    tive, theory/practice)
  - Identify who participated and how variables were measured
  - Identify limitations to be addressed in efforts to strengthen your
    research
- Synthesize the literature:
  - Avoid note card presentation and strive to represent an inte-
    grated body of knowledge
  - Use headings to organize your presentation
  - Introduce and summarize each section of the review
- Document the literature:
  - Move from very general to very specific representations of
    what is known
  - Explain inconsistencies
  - Use tables to compare, contrast, and summarize bodies of
    knowledge

ILLUSTRATIONS FROM PRACTICE

The following illustrations depict ways in which literature reviews help
guide the research process.

Illustration 1

To guide their study of the impact of school culture on school effectiveness, Rossman, Corbett, and Firestone (1984) examined literatures from

four traditions: anthropology, sociology, organization theory, and education. In addition, these researchers explored literature on cultural change and transformation, some of which had been applied to the study of organizations, and the literature on educational change and innovation. These traditions were used to develop the idea that change in school culture could be conceptualized as evolutionary, additive, or transformative. Further examination of the literature on educational innovation and implementation helped refine this into the idea that change initiatives might influence school culture. Finally, a search through the literature on successful schools and other types of organizations generated five domains that might exist in schools in the process of fundamental changes in their meaning structures. These researchers' efforts illustrated a creative use of literature outside the field of education and helped frame data collection for the research project (Rossman, 1985).

Illustration 2

Researching women's unequal representation in school administration careers, Marshall (1981) reviewed the work of previous researchers. Then, departing from tradition, Marshall examined the issue from the perspective of adult socialization and career socialization theory, including recruitment, training, and selection processes. With her knowledge of organizational theory that emphasized the influence of organizational norms and informal processes, Marshall was able to create a new research question and different research design. The literature review, therefore, helped determine the study's relevant concepts (i.e., norms, informal training, etc.) and shape the tentative guiding hypotheses. The literature review also established the significance of the research for practice and policy with an overview of the issues of affirmative action and gender equity.

CONTENT REVIEW

1. Why should a researcher be familiar with the literature that exists on her or his topic?
2. What are some benefits of doing a review of the literature?
3. In what ways does knowledge of the literature influence one's research efforts?

ACTIVITIES AND APPLICATIONS FOR
PROSPECTIVE RESEARCHERS

1. Locate a doctoral dissertation that uses case study research. What are the headings used in the literature review? Why do you think the dissertation's author used those headings?
2. Find a journal article that describes case study research. How would you assess the quality of the literature review in that article? How does this author's literature review help others identify viable and important research questions?
3. What literature would you read to prepare for your case study research project? How would knowledge of that literature influence your research efforts?

CHAPTER 5

Selecting a Design

Case study research designs or approaches can be based on their function, characteristics, or disciplinary perspective. One's selection of a research design is determined by how well it allows full investigation of a particular research question. Employed by researchers in the fields of psychology, sociology, education, medicine, law, political science, government, and business, case study designs are often related to the disciplinary background from which they are derived. Merriam (2001) suggests that case study research may be founded in *ethnographic, historical, psychological*, or *sociological* orientations. Case study research designs may also be classified as *intrinsic, instrumental*, or *collective* (Stake, 1995). Types of case study research designs include *exploratory, explanatory*, and *descriptive* (Yin, 2003).

One case study orientation is the *ethnographic* design. Originating in anthropology, ethnographic case study research is used when one wants to explore the observable and learned patterns of behavior, customs, and ways of life of a culture-sharing group. Ethnographic case studies typically involve extended interaction with the group, during which the researcher is immersed in the day-to-day lives of group members. The outgrowth of this effort is a holistic description of the group that incorporates both the views of group members and the researcher's perceptions and interpretations of the group's functioning. For example, a researcher may have interest in the culture of a school or a dynamic within a grade level or classroom. Ethnography succeeds if it teaches us how to behave appropriately in the cultural setting, whether it is in the office of a school principal or in a kindergarten classroom (Wolcott, 1973).

Another case study orientation is the *historical* analysis. Historical case studies are often descriptions of events, programs, or organizations as they have evolved over time. Extending traditional historical research, historical case study research typically includes direct observation and interviews of key participants. Historical case study research produces more than a chronological listing of events; it results in a researcher's descriptive interpretation of factors that both cause and result from the events. For example, a school superintendent might desire to evaluate schools that evolved out of the era of desegregation. Through a historical analysis study, the superintendent might uncover how the school came into being, what the first years were like, and changes that occurred over time involving urban school reorganization.

Examining literature and practices in psychology related to aspects of human behavior are common in *psychological* case study research. Although the individual is typically the focus of psychological case studies, organizations and programs as well as events are sometimes investigated using the theories and concepts generated by many years of research in psychology. For example, Piaget developed a theory of cognitive structure that has had an enormous impact on curriculum and instruction. A researcher's psychological case study of an elderly learner might draw upon Piaget's theory to help explain the learner's involvement in a patient education or training program (Merriam, 2001).

Topics often examined in *sociological* case study research include families, religion, politics, health care, demographics, urbanization, and issues related to gender, race, status, and aging. Sociological case study research, with its focus on society, social institutions, and social relationships, examines the structure, development, interaction, and collective behavior of organized groups of individuals. Case studies in education using a sociological perspective have explored student-teacher interactions, middle school social structures, and the impact of equity issues and student achievement (Lecompte & Preissle, 1993).

In addition to their disciplinary orientation, case study research designs may be classified as intrinsic, instrumental, or collective. Researchers engage in *intrinsic* case study research when they want to know more about a particular individual, group, event, or organization. Using an intrinsic case study, researchers are not necessarily interested in examining or creating general theories or in generalizing their findings to broader populations. For example, an intrinsic case study may occur when a teacher explores the extracurricular activities of a poorly performing student or when a nurse investigates an abnormally high infant mortality rate in the neonatal intensive care unit of a local hospital.

The primary goal of an *instrumental* case study research design is to better understand a theoretical question or problem. Using this approach, enhanced understanding of the particular issue being examined is of secondary importance to a greater insight of the theoretical explanation that underpins the issue. For example, a researcher may wish to better understand how college students acquire technology knowledge. Although the researcher's primary goal is to broaden our understanding of the processes and circumstances surrounding technology learning, insights may also be derived regarding specific instructional practices that support technology skill development.

Finally, *collective* case study research attempts to address an issue in question while adding to the literature base that helps us better conceptualize a theory. This design usually involves several instrumental cases performed to enhance our ability to theorize about some larger collection of cases. For example, a researcher may engage in a series of studies designed to explore one of the seven intelligence forms contained in Gardner's (1999) theory of multiple intelligence. Findings from these studies may substantiate the theory while simultaneously providing insights into how people think and behave in a particular situation.

Three types of case study research designs include *exploratory, explanatory*, and *descriptive*. Exploratory designs seek to define research questions of a subsequent study or to determine the feasibility of research procedures. These designs are often a prelude to additional research efforts and involve fieldwork and information collection prior to the definition of a research question. For example, before assuming her new position, an incoming business executive may conduct an exploratory study of her company's ethical climate to determine how business practices normally occur. Explanatory designs seek to establish cause-and-effect relationships. Their primary purpose is to determine how events occur and which ones may influence particular outcomes. For example, a middle school teacher may conduct an explanatory case study to identify factors in his students' home environments that affect their classroom performance. Finally, descriptive designs attempt to present a complete description of a phenomenon within its context. An example may be a hospital administrator who attempts to gain a thorough description of her hospital's emergency room procedures when admitting incoming patients.

Doing case study research means selecting a design that matches the disciplinary perspective of the investigation. Ethnographic designs are used to study targeted interactions of a group; historical designs focus on events or programs as they change over time; psychological designs are used to study human behavior in detail; and sociological designs are used for case study research that addresses broad issues in society, social institutions, and social relationships. Intrinsic designs focus on a particular individual, event, situation, program, or activity. An instrumental design is used to better understand a theory or problem. A collective design is used to understand a theory or problem by combining information from smaller cases. When the design is identified, the next step is gathering information using interviews, observations, and documents.

RELATIONS BETWEEN DESIGN AND METHOD

Different designs or approaches to case study research represent different general assumptions about methods and sources of data. Of course, any method can be used in any type of research and multiple methods are often used when doing case study research, but relationships between design and method are a foundation for planning a successful investigation (see Table 5.1).

ILLUSTRATIONS FROM PRACTICE

Illustration 1: Intrinsic

The following illustration depicts an *intrinsic* case study in which our focus is to learn more about a particular individual, group, event, or organization and less about examining/creating general theories or generalizing research findings to broader populations.

Kalnins (1986) sought to examine in depth the contexts, processes, and interactions within long-term health-care facilities that shape the residents' views of life. Using a variety of case study data collection strategies, Kalnins anticipated that participant observation and interviewing would run concurrently, producing data with which to substantiate

Table 5.1. Relationships Between Design and Method

Design	Method
Ethnographic approaches are grounded in firsthand experience.	Interviews[1] Observations[2]
Historical approaches are grounded in representing and interpreting records, papers, and other sources of information about people, phenomena, or practices.	Document analyses[3] Interviews
Psychological approaches are grounded in personal experiences and ways of looking at the world.	Interviews Observations
Sociological approaches are grounded in the structure, development, interaction, and collective behavior of organized groups of individuals.	Interviews Observations

[1] See chapter 6 for information on interviews.
[2] See chapter 7 for information on observations.
[3] See chapter 8 for information on document analyses.

events, explore emerging hypotheses, and make further decisions about the conduct of the research. She reasoned that this approach would allow identification of everyday actions and interactions about complex social structures in order to accomplish her major research purpose—to understand the meanings given to events by residents in long-term health-care facilities.

Illustration 2: Instrumental

The following illustration depicts an *instrumental* case study in which we want to better understand a theoretical explanation that underpins a particular issue more than we want to understand the issue itself.

In an instrumental case study, Kincannon (2002) described the experience of university faculty as they redesigned face-to-face classroom instruction for a Web-based environment. Participants were faculty members from a major research institution in the southeastern United States. To identify faculty perceptions beyond those represented by the participants, the participants were selected to represent a range of experiences and viewpoints toward distance education and teaching styles. Data collection involved interviews, a document review, class observations, and a focus group. The findings documented the effects of Web-based technology on the perceptions of faculty regarding their teaching roles, experiences, and workplace context. The implications for instructional design support in other settings were examined.

Illustration 3: Collective

The following illustration addresses an issue while simultaneously adding to the literature base that helps us better conceptualize a theory. This design usually involves several instrumental cases selected to allow an enhanced ability to theorize about some larger collection of cases.

Crudden (2002) used a collective case study approach to examine factors that influenced the job retention of persons with vision loss. It was found that computer technology was a major positive influence and that print access and technology were sources of stress for most participants. A qualitative data collection process was used to facilitate an in-depth understanding of the rehabilitation process for persons who retained employment after vision loss. This approach allowed the reader to gain insight into the rehabilitation process, from the consumer's perspective. The collective case study method allowed for greater understanding of a phenomenon, in this case job retention, to facilitate theorizing for a larger collection of cases.

Illustration 4: Ethnographic

The following two illustrations of *ethnographic* case studies involved extended interaction with the group, during which the researcher was immersed in the day-to-day lives of group members, the outgrowth of which was a holistic description of the group that incorporated both the views of group members and the researcher's perceptions and interpretations of the group's functioning.

Thorne (1993) reported that a researcher regularly visited a multicultural public elementary school where she spent long periods of time observing and listening carefully to boys and girls as they performed their day-to-day activities in the classroom, on the playground, in the gym, in the lunchroom, and in other less supervised places. She was studying how children experience gender in school. The book that resulted from her work is rich in detail regarding gender interaction among groups of children.

Illustration 5: Ethnographic

In Adler and Adler's (1991) study, a man and a woman sat in a packed athletic stadium watching a men's collegiate basketball game. Although it was difficult to distinguish them from other enthusiastic spectators, these were researchers engaged in a study of the socialization and education of male college athletes. Attending games was only one part of their research work. They also interviewed players, athletic staff, boosters, the athletes' women friends, media personnel, and professors and collected press reports and other written materials related to the team and players.

Illustration 6: Historical

The following illustration is a historical case study that depicts a researcher's descriptive interpretation of factors that both caused and resulted from events surrounding the historical evolution of one organization.

While many studies have highlighted the struggles of corporate America as it attempts to embrace a "green" marketing orientation, few studies have explored the attempts of environmental organizations to market their messages. The intent of Lankard and McLaughlin's (2003) historical case study research was to identify and describe core messages used by one national environmental organization, the Wilderness Society (TWS), to promote forest conservation from 1964 to 2000. The findings demonstrated that TWS consistently applied elements of marketing in its promotion of forest conservation and had a strategic approach to developing and maintaining continuity with its messages. This new knowledge helped researchers understand the particulars of the historical and current use of marketing within one leading U.S. environmental organization.

Illustration 7: Psychological

The following two illustrations of *psychological* case study research examine literature and practices in psychology related to aspects of human behavior.

Hook (2003) examined the progression and ultimate dissolution of a developmental psychopathology research project on a notorious serial killer. This detailed case study outlined a classical psychoanalytic interpretation of the killer's psychopathology through the interlocking accounts of the zonal stages, the Oedipus complex, and the id/ego/superego structural dynamics of personality. This and other similar regularizing engagements with the topic were then themselves analyzed and critiqued as producing multiple lines of objectification, fictionalization, prurience, and distance. By way of resolution, the study listed a series of concerns about particular trends of attempted knowledge production in psychology.

Illustration 8: Psychological

Utsey, Howard, and Williams (2003) presented a therapeutic mentoring group model for working with at-risk, urban African American male adolescents to reduce self-destructive behaviors (e.g., drug use, gang activity, sexual promiscuity, self/other directed violence) and to encourage more socially adaptive behaviors. Using a case study approach, the researchers described the model's implementation and its clinical utility with this population. The findings demonstrated the utility of this unique and culturally congruent approach to working with a population historically underserved by the mental health profession.

Illustration 9: Sociological

The following illustration depicts some of the topics (e.g., families, religion, politics, health care, demographics, urbanization, and issues related to gender, race, status, and aging) that are often examined in *sociological* case study research.

Salamon (2003) reviewed sociologists' and anthropologists' holistic descriptions of American rural communities since post–World War II. Three community case studies were briefly sketched—one of an agrarian community in slow decline, another of a postagrarian community where suburbanization was overwhelming agrarian traits, and a third of a community that combined elements of both. The author noted that regional suburbanization processes are transforming rural America socially and physically, threatening the uniqueness of small towns, whose diversity is a national resource. He argued that the loss of place attachment and community identity have had particularly negative effects on youth, whose socialization has become privatized as parental civic engagement and general adult watchfulness decline. These changes constitute a community effect for rural youth analogous to the neighborhood effect richly documented by urban sociologists for inner-city youth. He concluded that small towns should attempt to resist homogenization of the vital aspects of agrarian community life they most cherish.

CONTENT REVIEW

1. What case study research designs and orientations are employed typically by researchers? How do these designs differ?
2. What are the differences and similarities between the intrinsic, instrumental, and collective classifications of research designs?

ACTIVITIES AND APPLICATIONS FOR
PROSPECTIVE RESEARCHERS

1. Find three articles that describe case study research. What design is used in each research effort? Why might the authors have chosen this design?
2. Historical case study orientations often describe the evolution of events, programs, or organizations. What would be some advantages and disadvantages of using historical analysis to research how administrators (e.g., schools, businesses, nonprofit organizations) spend their time?
3. Which research orientation and design might be appropriate for your case study research project? Why?

CHAPTER 6

Gathering Information from Interviews

Having identified a disciplinary orientation and design for the investigation, a researcher gathers information that will address the fundamental research question. Interviews are a very common form of data collection in case study research. Interviews of individuals or groups allow the researcher to attain rich, personalized information (Mason, 2002). To conduct a successful interview, the researcher should follow several guidelines.

First, the researcher should identify key participants in the situation whose knowledge and opinions may provide important insights regarding the research questions. Participants may be interviewed individually or in groups. Individual interviews yield significant amounts of information from an individual's perspective, but may be quite time-consuming. Group interviews capitalize on the sharing and creation of new ideas that sometimes would not occur if the participants were interviewed individually; however, group interviews run the risk of not fully capturing all participants' viewpoints. A teacher exploring factors that influence student attrition in her school would need to weigh the advantages and disadvantages of interviewing individually or collectively selected students, teachers, administrators, and even the students' parents.

Second, the researcher should develop an interview guide (sometimes called an interview protocol). This guide will identify appropriate open-ended questions that the researcher will ask each interviewee. These questions are designed to allow the researcher to gain insights into the study's fundamental research questions; hence, the quantity of interview questions for a particular interview varies widely. For example, a nurse interested in his hospital's potentially discriminatory employment practices may write questions for his hospital's chief administrator that include, What qualifications do you seek in your employees? How do you ensure that you hire the most qualified candidates for positions in your hospital? and How does your hospital serve ethnic minorities?

Third, the researcher should consider the setting in which he or she conducts the interview. Although interviews in the natural setting may enhance realism, the researcher may seek a private, neutral, and distraction-free interview location to increase the comfort of the interviewee and the likelihood of attaining high-quality information. For example, a technology specialist exploring her organization's computer software adoption procedures may elect to question her company's administrators in a separate office rather than in the presence of coworkers.

Fourth, the researcher should develop a means for recording the interview data. Handwritten notes sometimes suffice, but the lack of detail associated with this approach inevitably results in a loss of valuable information. The best way to record interview data is to audiotape the interaction. Before audiotaping, however, the researcher must obtain the participant's permission. After the interview, the researcher transcribes the recording for closer scrutiny and comparison with data derived from other sources.

Fifth, the researcher must adhere to legal and ethical requirements for all research involving people. Interviewees should not be deceived and are protected from any form of mental, physical, or emotional injury. Interviewees must provide informed consent for their participation in the research. Unless otherwise required by law or unless interviewees consent to public identification, information attained from an interview should be anonymous and confidential. Interviewees have the right to end the interview and should be debriefed by the case study researcher after the research has ended.

Interviews may be structured, semistructured, or unstructured. Semistructured interviews are particularly well-suited for case study research. Using this approach, researchers ask predetermined but flexibly worded questions, the answers to which provide tentative answers to the researchers' questions. In addition to posing predetermined questions, researchers using semistructured interviews ask follow-up questions designed to probe more deeply issues of interest to interviewees. In this manner, semistructured interviews invite interviewees to express themselves openly and freely and to define the world from their own perspectives, not solely from the perspective of the researcher.

Identifying and gaining access to interviewees is a critical step. Selection of interviewees directly influences the quality of the information attained. Although availability is important, this should not be the only criterion for selecting interviewees. The most important consideration is to identify those persons in the research setting who may have the best information with which to address the study's research questions. Those potential interviewees must be willing to participate in an interview. The researcher must have the ability and resources with which to gain access to the interviewees.

When conducting an interview, a researcher should accomplish several tasks. First, she should ensure that she attains the consent of the interviewee to proceed with the interview and clarify issues of anonymity and confidentiality. Second, she should review with the interviewee the purpose of the interview, the approximate amount of time needed for the interview, and how and when the interviewee may expect to receive results of the research of which this interview is a part. While asking questions, the researcher should ask only open-ended questions (e.g., What factors enhance productivity in this organization?) while avoiding yes/no questions (e.g., Are you happy with your job?), leading questions (e.g., How long have you disliked your boss?) or multiple-part questions (e.g., How do you feel about your coworkers and your bosses?). Finally, the researcher should remember that time spent *talking* to the interviewee would be better spent *listening* to the interviewee. In other words, the researcher should limit her comments as much as possible to allow more time for the interviewee to offer his perspectives.

Interviews are frequently used when doing case study research. Some guidelines for use when doing interviews are presented in Tables 6.1–6.3. Table 6.1 outlines how to plan and conduct an interview. Table 6.2 describes variations in interview instrumentation. Table 6.3 identifies interview questions to avoid. Typically, key participants provide answers to questions focused on areas being investigated (e.g., knowledge of block scheduling, reasons that students drop out of school, opinions about employment practices). The researcher is guided by an interview guide and conducts the interview in a setting chosen to maximize the responsiveness of those being interviewed. Responses are written down or electronically recorded for later review and analysis. When conducting interviews, researchers are careful not to violate legal or ethical protections. While interviews are widely used, other methods are also used to gather data in case study research.

ILLUSTRATION FROM PRACTICE

A local school district has lost 8 of its 31 principals and assistant principals during the past 2 years. A case study researcher (CSR) interviews the school district superintendent (SDS) to determine his perceptions of the reasons for the departures. After tape-recording the interview, the CSR transcribes the contents of the interview. A portion of the transcribed interview appears below.

Table 6.1. How to Plan and Conduct an Interview

Step	Action	Example
1.	List the research questions that your study will explore.	What happens during a transition from traditional to block scheduling?
2.	Break research questions into researchable subquestions.	I. What do teachers do differently when block scheduling is implemented? II. What do students do differently when block scheduling is implemented?
3.	Develop possible interview topics or items for each subquestion.	I.1. What new activities do teachers use when implementing block scheduling? I.2. What do teachers do differently during the beginning, middle, and end of block-scheduled classes? II.1. How do students spend their time during block-scheduled classes? II.2. What do students think about block scheduling?
4.	Cross-reference interview topics or items with each research question to ensure that nothing is overlooked.	Two topics have been identified for each research question. Additional topics may evolve as interview protocol is formalized.
5.	Develop interview structure (i.e., format) and protocol (i.e., guide) for interviews.	*Structure*: Each "subject" will be asked the same set of questions in the same order at the end of the first year of block scheduling. *Protocol (Teachers)*: 1. How long have you been teaching? 2. What grade do you teach? 3. What did the block schedule allow you to do that you could not do on the traditional schedule? 4. What did you do differently in the first year of block scheduling? 5. What are the advantages of block scheduling? 6. What are the disadvantages of block scheduling?
6.	Identify minimum information to be gathered from each respondent.	Each respondent will provide demographic information (Questions 1–2) and a response to Questions 3 and 4; other questions are optional.
7.	Confirm appropriateness and adequacy of protocol and conduct interview.	Research questions can be answered with completed interviews.

Adapted from J. Mason. (2002). *Qualitative researching* (2nd ed.). Thousand Oaks, CA: Sage.

Table 6.2. Variations in Interview Instrumentation

Type of Interview	Characteristics	Strengths	Weaknesses
Interview as informal conversation	Questions are derived from the ongoing context and are asked in the course of interview and there are no predetermined questions, topics, or wording.	Value and relevance of questions is heightened, topics are built on and emerge from observations, and the questions can be matched to individuals and circumstances.	Information may be different when collected from different people using different questions. May be less systematic and comprehensive if particular questions do not arise. Data organization and systematic analysis may be difficult.
Interview as guided conversation	Information to be addressed is specified in advance, but interviewer defines the sequence and wording of questions during the course of the interview.	The plan increases the completeness of the data and makes data collection more systematic for each participant, potential gaps in process can be anticipated and addressed, and interviews remain conversational and situational.	Critical topics may be inadvertently missed. Flexibility in sequencing and wording questions may result in different responses from different participants and may reduce the comparability of responses.
Interview as open-ended responses	Specific wording and sequence of questions are predetermined, all participants are asked basic questions in the same order, and all questions require open-ended responses.	Comparability of responses may be strengthened, completeness of data for each person is enhanced, effects of interviewer biases are minimized, and analysis and organization are facilitated.	Flexibility is limited for relating the interview to specific individuals and circumstances. The standardized wording of the questions may limit variation in answers.
Interview as fixed responses	Questions and responses options are predetermined, response options are fixed, and respondent selects appropriate response.	Data analysis is simplified, responses can be compared and combined, and a larger number of questions can be addressed in a brief space and time.	Experiences and perceptions are fit to predetermined categories. Often perceived as impersonal, irrelevant, and mechanical. Meaning or richness of experiences may be distorted by limiting response options.

Adapted from M. Q. Patton. (2002). *Qualitative research and evaluation methods* (3rd ed.). Newbury Park, CA: Sage.

Table 6.3. Interview Questions to Avoid

Type	Example
Questions with multiple answers	How do you feel about your teachers and courses?
Questions with leading answers	What social problems have you had since you began working here?
Questions with uninformative answers	Do you like the course? Do you like this job?

Adapted from S. B. Merriam. (1988). *Case study research in education: A qualitative approach.* San Francisco: Jossey-Bass.

Time/Date: 1:30 p.m., November 2, 2005
Location: Superintendent's Office

CSR: Thank you again for agreeing to meet with me.

SDS: My pleasure.

CSR: As I stated on the telephone, I am interested in your views regarding why several school administrators have left your district during the past 2 years.

SDS: Many reasons . . . most of which are very understandable.

CSR: Such as?

SDS: Two school principals left because of opportunities in other school districts. One received a promotion to associate superintendent in another state . . . The other got a job as a principal in a larger school system where she could make more money. Both were excellent employees and I was sorry to lose them, but I never stand in the way of someone who wants to move up . . . Another principal reached mandatory retirement age and had to step down . . . He was an excellent administrator, too. *[Silence]*

CSR: My review of your district's records indicates that five other administrators left the district, also. What were their reasons for leaving?

SDS: Well, I thought there were only four other departures . . . I'll have to look into that. Anyway, one principal retired . . . a bit early, I think . . . I'm not sure why . . . I think he was just tired of it all. And I recall that one of our assistant principals left to start his own business . . . in computer programming, I believe. And . . . um, let me see, oh yes . . . one assistant principal left to have a baby and never came back . . .

CSR: Why did she not return?

SDS: Not sure . . . I should probably look into that, also. I heard someone say that she had some complications in delivery.

CSR: You mentioned that you were aware of four other departures. You have named only three . . . why did the other person leave?

SDS: He had some . . . well, shall I say . . . problems. He seemed overly attracted to a couple of teachers in his school and they complained. At first I moved him to another school . . . you know, to give him another chance. But it seemed that his reputation followed him so he eventually left.

CSR: To what extent was his departure voluntary?

SDS: Completely . . . he was a good worker . . . he just had a rough start at his first school.

CSR: I see . . .

CONTENT REVIEW

1. What guidelines should a researcher follow to conduct a successful interview?
2. Why might it be important to develop an interview guide *before* conducting an interview?

ACTIVITIES AND APPLICATIONS FOR PROSPECTIVE RESEARCHERS

1. Locate a research study in which an interview is used to gather information. What questions are included in the interview guide? Are the questions useful for gathering information with which to address the study's research question(s)?
2. Locate a thesis or dissertation in which an interview is used to gather information. Could the questions or setting in which the questions are asked be improved? How?
3. What questions might be included in an interview guide with which to gather information about the levels of knowledge of professors about case study research?
4. For your case study research project, whom do you plan to interview? What five or six questions might you include on your interview guide for each interviewee? How do you plan to record the information obtained during the interviews?

CHAPTER 7

Gathering Information from Observations

A frequent source of information in case study research is observations of the research setting by the researcher. Unlike interviews, which rely on people's sometimes biased perceptions and recollections of events, observations of the setting by a case study researcher may provide more objective information related to the research topic. However, conducting meaningful observations requires skill and persistence.

The researcher should consider five factors when conducting observations. The most important factor is for the researcher to identify what must be observed in order to shed light on possible answers to the research questions. For example, an administrator interested in the effects of block scheduling may keep track of the number and kind of discipline referrals that occur before and after using the approach in several schools. A teacher who wants to identify factors that influence student attrition may decide to observe students' behaviors and achievement in classrooms in which teachers implement different instructional strategies. A nurse interested in his hospital's employment practices may want to watch the human resource officer interview several candidates for various hospital positions. A technology specialist investigating her organization's software adoption procedures may ask to observe meetings of corporate administrators during which judgments are made about computer software capabilities.

Second, similar to the interview guide, a case study researcher should create an observation guide—a list of features to be addressed during a particular observation. This list often includes the time/date/location of the observation, names/positions of persons being observed, specific activities and events related to the research questions, and initial impressions and interpretations of the activities and events under observation.

Third, a case study researcher must gain access to the research setting. Anticipating that participants in the setting may be suspicious of the researcher's goals, the researcher must be prepared to explain why, how, and for whom the investigation is occurring. Toward that end, the researcher should seek the trust of the participants and strive to be as unobtrusive as possible.

Fourth, the researcher must recognize his or her personal role and biases related to the research. Unlike other forms of research in which the researcher attempts to maintain distance from the setting and activities, case study researchers are usually immersed in their work. As a result, if not recognized and addressed, these researchers' inherent biases and predispositions may prejudice their activities and interpretations of the study's findings. Case study researchers must actively attempt to identify and mitigate the effects of their biases and prejudices in order to ensure the impartiality of their conclusions.

Fifth, a case study researcher must follow all ethical and legal requirements regarding research participants. Researchers are required by federal law to minimize risks, to balance any risks with potential benefits of the research, and to inform participants of any risks involved. As is the case with individuals being interviewed in case study research, persons being observed must provide informed consent of their participation in the research and are normally afforded anonymity and confidentiality. Individuals who are observed have the right to end an observation and should be debriefed after the research has ended to ensure that no mental, physical, or psychological injury has occurred.

Observations are frequently used in the course of case study research. Typically, observations provide answers to questions being investigated (e.g., instructional approaches used by teachers during block scheduling, how students who drop out of school spend their time, frequency of different employment practices). The researcher develops an observation guide and conducts the observation in a setting chosen to maximize the usefulness of data that are gathered. Responses are systematically recorded for later review and analysis. When conducting observations, researchers are careful not to violate legal or ethical protections. While observations are widely used, other methods are also used to gather data in case study research.

DESIGN ILLUSTRATIONS

Observation notes must be specific. Two ways to record observations are illustrated in Table 7.1. In the left-hand column, the notes are vague and overgeneralized; in the right-hand column, the notes from the same observation are detailed and concrete.

Table 7.1. Examples of Proper and Improper Notes

Vague and Overgeneralized Notes	Detailed and Concrete Notes
1. The student appeared uneasy as he arrived for his first day of school.	The young boy stood motionless at the door to the kindergarten classroom. He looked nervously at the teacher and then at the children near him. His eyes were watery and a bead of sweat was on his upper lip. He gripped the left strap of his backpack so tightly that his fingers were turning pale. Twice, he opened his mouth as if to speak, but no words came out. When asked by the teacher if he would like to join the class, he took two small steps backward and shook his head no.
2. The student seemed to relax a bit on the playground.	At recess, the boy burst from the door of the school and ran excitedly to the monkey bars on the playground. He swung upside down for about 2 minutes before jumping to the ground. Although still not talking to anyone, he rapidly climbed the ladder of the tallest slide. At the top of the ladder, he suddenly smiled broadly for the first time that day.
3. Later on, the student started to get into his schoolwork.	During afternoon centers, the boy selected the computer station. He sat down and, without prompting, turned on the computer. After a minute of running his hands over the computer, monitor, and keyboard, he turned to the teacher and asked softly, "Do you have Wonder World on here?" When the teacher showed him how to click on Wonder World, the boy worked intently with the software program for the remainder of the period. On occasion, he quietly demonstrated verbal expressions of glee and excitement with words such as *wow, super,* and *"sweet."*
4. The student was happy at the end of the day.	At 2:15 p.m., the boy climbed aboard the bus with a huge smile on his face. He bantered with two schoolmates, laughed loudly at a joke offered by the bus driver, and pushed his face against the bus window while waving feverishly at his teacher as the bus drove away.

ILLUSTRATIONS FROM PRACTICE

Illustration 1: Hints for Writing Observation Notes

(Adapted from R. C. Bogden & S. K. Bilken. [2003]. *Qualitative research in education: An introduction to theories and methods* [4th ed.]. New York: Allyn and Bacon.)

1. Do it right away and don't put it off because the more time that passes, the harder it will be to recall important details and complete the task.
2. Talk about an observation after you record it, not before, because the conversation may cloud the recollection of what occurred.
3. Work in a location free from distractions.
4. Assign sufficient time to complete the task in one session; when in doubt, allocate more time rather than less.
5. Start with notes and an outline reflecting key parts of the observation and fill in details as you complete the task.
6. Try to capture the events in the same order in which they occurred.
7. Let your notes reflect what you are thinking and write your thoughts down on paper; if it helps, "talk through" what happened as you prepare your notes.
8. If you notice something is missing as you are writing or after you have finished, just add it to your notes; if you notice something that should be deleted or changed, just do it.
9. Keep in mind that the benefits of careful note-taking can pay big dividends later in your study.

Illustration 2: Example of Observation Guiding Questions

(Adapted from J. W. Creswell. [2002]. *Educational research: Planning, conducting, and evaluating quantitative and qualitative research.* Upper Saddle River, NJ: Prentice Hall.)

Participant(s) and setting(s)?
Individual conducting observation?
Role of the observer (participant, nonparticipant, other)?
Time, place, and length of observation?
Descriptive observations? (individuals, setting descriptors)?
Reflections (experiences, hypotheses, guidance)?

CONTENT REVIEW

1. Why is observation one of the best forms of data collection in case study research?
2. What factors should a researcher consider in order to successfully observe a research setting?

ACTIVITIES AND APPLICATIONS FOR
PROSPECTIVE RESEARCHERS

1. Locate a research article in which observations are used to gather information. What is observed in this study? Is there evidence that the researchers adhered to factors for conducting successful observations?
2. Locate a thesis or dissertation in which observations are used to gather information. Do the observations gather information with which to address the study's research questions?
3. What settings might you observe to gather information related to your research project? What observation factors discussed in this chapter might you consider when planning your observation of each setting?

CHAPTER 8

Gathering Information from Documents

In addition to using interviews and observations, case study researchers often review existing documents or create and administer new documents from which to gather information related to the research questions. Documents take many forms and often vary in usefulness. A thorough researcher gathers information from as many relevant documents as possible. When planning to use documents, the researcher asks: *Who* has the information? *What* part of it is needed? *Where* is it? *When* was it prepared? *How* will it be collected? The results of document analyses are often summarized in narrative form or integrated into tables that illustrate trends and other significant outcomes. Documents examined by a case study researcher include material extracted from the Internet, private and public records, physical evidence, and instruments created by the researcher.

Internet sources vary greatly in quality and reliability. Although their physical attractiveness and complexity may make many sites on the Internet appear valid, a prudent researcher determines the authenticity and legitimacy of an Internet source before relying on information derived from that source. For example, a technology specialist may determine that information derived from the home page of a nationally recognized technology organization is more reputable than is information encountered in a local technology company's Web site.

Private and public records are another potentially useful source of information. Private records include any material produced by an individual that provides insights into the person's beliefs, attitudes, and behaviors. Examples include personal letters, notes, diaries, and family pictures. Public records are documents that reflect beliefs, attitudes, and behaviors beyond those of a particular individual. These documents may include court records, licenses, and certificates of birth, marriage, and death. A teacher investigating factors that influence student attrition may discover that a particular student's diary entries combined with local police reports provide explanatory evidence for that student's unexpected departure from school.

Another source of information with which to address a case study researcher's questions may be physical evidence. This category of information includes anything physical that is associated with the case under investigation. For example, a nurse interested in his hospital's potentially discriminatory employment practices may compare the number of ethnic minorities on the medical staff with the number of ethnic minorities on the custodial staff. A technology specialist investigating her company's software adoption practices may examine the types of software programs used most frequently by her colleagues. A teacher researching student attrition may observe the number and types of after-school academic and sports activities in which his school's students participate.

Instruments created by the researcher often provide a powerful means by which to collect information pertaining to the researcher's questions. These instruments may include surveys, questionnaires, and examinations administered to individuals who have insight into the research situation. An advantage of this category is that instruments created by the researcher can be designed to address the specific research questions in need of investigation. A potential disadvantage is that these instruments are primarily self-report measures—research reveals that people do not always portray themselves truthfully when they are asked to respond to surveys, questionnaires, and examinations (Creswell, 1998; Glesne & Peshkin, 1992; Hatch, 2002).

These four categories of documents—the Internet, private and public records, physical evidence, and instruments created by the researcher—are not mutually exclusive. When used separately or in conjunction, they provide a rich source of information with which to augment data collected through interviews and observations.

The analysis of documents is a commonly used method in case study research. If you decide to use documentary evidence, you should have a clear view for why this method is appropriate (e.g., available information provides meaningful answers to your research questions). You should also have access to key documents and a well-developed plan for analyzing them. When combined with information from interviews and observations, information gleaned from documents provides the case study researcher with important information from multiple data sources that must be summarized and interpreted in order to address the research questions under investigation.

AUTHENTICITY OF DOCUMENTS

Clark (1967) suggests asking the following questions regarding documents used in a case study:

- Where has the document been and what is its history?
- How did the document become available (public domain, special considerations)?
- What guarantee exists that the document is appropriate, accurate, and timely?
- Is the integrity of the document without concern?
- Has the document been changed in any way?
- Is the document representative under the conditions and for the purposes it was produced?
- Who created the document and with what intention (potential bias)?
- What were the sources of information (original source, secondary data, other) used to create the document?
- Do other sources exist that can be used to confirm the information in the document? (pp. 238–239).

QUESTIONS TO ANSWER WHEN GATHERING INFORMATION FROM DOCUMENTS

- What sources (e.g., written records, reports, charts, graphs, tables) are available that can be used to provide answers to my research questions?
- What types of answers (i.e., literal or interpretive) will be available if the documents are used?
- How will information be selected from all that is available (i.e., universal or sampling set)?
- How will the information be collected (e.g., exact copy and/or data collection form)?
- How will documents be represented as answers to research questions (e.g., description, analysis, or interpretation)?
- What ethical concerns are relevant with regard to documents that will be analyzed?
- How will ethical concerns be addressed?

ILLUSTRATIONS FROM PRACTICE

Illustration 1

Merriam, S. B. (2001). *Qualitative research and case study applications in education*. San Francisco: Jossey-Bass.

If you were interested in studying the role of parent involvement in a neighborhood school, you could look for public-record documents in the form of the following: notices sent home to parents, memos between teachers, staff and the parents' association, formal policy statements regarding parent involvement, school bulletin boards or their displays featuring aspects of parent involvement, newspaper and other media coverage of activities featuring parent involvement, and any official records of parent attendance or presence in the school.

An entire study can be based on personal documents. Abramson's (1992) case study of Russian Jewish emigration is based solely on his grandfather's diaries, written over a 12-year period. A well-known earlier study of Polish immigrant life relied heavily upon personal letters written between immigrants and relatives in Europe (Thomas & Znaniecki, 1927). Many of these letters were obtained through appeals in ads placed in local newspapers.

Illustration 2

Benton-Kupper, J. (1999). Can less be more? The quantity versus quality issue of curriculum in a block schedule. *Journal of Research and Development in Education, 32*(3), 168–177.

In this case study, the experiences of three English teachers were examined during the 2nd year of transition from a high school traditional seven-period day schedule (43-minute periods) to a four-period day schedule (87-minute periods). The study addressed three questions: (1) How do English teachers describe their instructional strategies in a block schedule? (2) How do English teachers describe how they plan and prepare for a block schedule? and (3) How do English teachers describe the content taught in a block schedule? The primary form of data collection consisted of one interview with each participant, which was audiotaped with each participant's permission. Open-ended questions focused on the three main topics listed above, and participants were encouraged to discuss their experiences in depth. In addition to interviews, each teacher was observed twice so that the researcher could experience firsthand how the classrooms functioned. Each observation lasted the entire 87 minutes, with the researcher's field notes providing the primary data used to verify information collected in the participant interviews. The third form of data collection involved obtaining documents from the participants, including course syllabi, lesson plans, assignment handouts, and informational handouts, which were also used to validate interview data.

CONTENT REVIEW

1. What categories of documents do case study researchers use to obtain information with which to address their research questions?
2. What are some examples of public versus private records?

ACTIVITIES AND APPLICATIONS FOR
PROSPECTIVE RESEARCHERS

1. Locate a research study in which documents are used to gather information. What documents are used to derive answers to the researchers' questions? How useful are these documents? What other documents might have been used?
2. What documents might be used in a study of university library usage? Explain.
3. What documents might you use to gather information with which to address questions in your case study research project? Why might it be useful to collect information from multiple categories of documents and from more than one source of information?

CHAPTER 9

Summarizing and Interpreting the Information

In case study research, making sense of information collected from multiple sources is a recursive process in which the researcher interacts with the information throughout the investigative process. In other words, unlike some forms of research in which the data are examined only at the end of the information collection period, case study research involves ongoing examination and interpretation of the data in order to reach tentative conclusions and to refine the research questions. Case study researchers adhere to several guidelines as they simultaneously summarize and interpret information gathered when doing case study research.

One guideline involves ongoing refinement of the study's fundamental research questions in light of data obtained early in the investigation. For example, a teacher interested in factors that contribute to student attrition may discern from initial observations of her school's classrooms that teachers who rely strictly on lecture have the highest student drop-out rates. As a result, she may refine her initial question from, What factors contribute to student attrition? to, Why are attrition rates higher in classrooms in which teachers lecture exclusively?

Another guideline suggests constant focus on the research questions being investigated. A case study researcher can feel overwhelmed by the large amount of information normally obtained from interviews, observations, and documents. For example, a nurse exploring his hospital's employment practices may generate 300 pages of transcribed interview data, several dozen pages of field notes describing observations of his hospital, and a number of pieces of potentially relevant physical evidence. A way to control the resulting sense of helplessness is to constantly remind oneself of the fundamental research questions being explored in the study. Each new piece of information should be examined in light of these fundamental questions.

A third guideline involves collection and interpretation of only those data that are potentially meaningful to the research effort. Although premature elimination of potential information sources may lessen a case study researcher's ability to gain a complete explanation for the issues in the case, focusing on irrelevant information is equally counterproductive. For example, a technology specialist seeking insights into her company's software adoption policies may gain no useful information from her interviews of vendors of various software packages. As a result, she should not spend an inordinate amount of time reflecting on the vendor's comments.

Another guideline is to develop a method for labeling, storing, and gaining access to information acquired during the research effort. As a minimum, every piece of information gathered must be labeled with the date, location, persons involved, and circumstances surrounding the collection of that piece of information. A researcher may want to include additional information, such as his or her initial interpretations of the information. Although creation of a sound information management system may seem simplistic and its implementation laborious, the absence of such a system will jeopardize a researcher's ability to interpret the vast amount of information accumulated in a case study research project.

A final guideline involves the use of all available resources that can assist in the collection and interpretation of information. Independent experts may provide valuable guidance and opinions regarding the meaning of the information acquired. In recent years, computer software programs, such as NUDIST and The Ethnograph, have been created that may contribute to a case study researcher's ability to categorize and process large amounts of information. Although the viability of these software programs is not completely known, their potential seems limitless.

A key aspect of doing case study research is summarizing and interpreting information as a basis for understanding the topic being investigated. Typically, this process involves examining and reexamining research questions and answers that evolve as information becomes available for analysis. When information that is collected defines new questions, the case study researcher adjusts ongoing and subsequent methods and procedures. At the same time, efforts are made to keep an eye on the prize, that is, to keep fundamental research question(s) at the forefront of the investigative process. The nature of summarizing and interpreting information also sometimes means putting aside less relevant information as well as developing a management system for keeping track of all information that is used or not used.

Figure 9.1. Checklist for Implementing Case Study Methods

Research Questions	What Information Do I Need?	How Will I Gather the Information?	Why Is the Method Appropriate?	Other Information

DESIGN ILLUSTRATION: THINKING ABOUT METHOD

Charts can provide a means of checking the adequacy of a researcher's thinking throughout the research process. Completing the chart in Figure 9.1 will help you focus on the methodology that underlies your research.

ILLUSTRATIONS FROM PRACTICE

Illustration 1

We recommend using a systematic procedure to make analysis of field notes and other forms of data more manageable. Berg (2004, p. 286) provides the "model" shown in Figure 9.2 as an illustration of the content analysis process.

Illustration 2

What counts in interpreting information? The task of classifying and interpreting large amounts of information typically available in data that are gathered as part of intensive case study research can be made more manageable by quantifying different components of the collected information. According to Berg (2004), the following elements can be counted in most written messages:

> *Words*: These are the smallest element used in content analysis. The uses are generally associated with frequency of specified words or terms.

Themes: These are more useful than words to count. In its most basic form, a theme is a simple sentence, a string of words with a subject and a predicate. A researcher may be well served to count every time a theme is provided or he or she may simply point one out in a paragraph or section analysis.

Characters: The number of times a person or persons are mentioned can be very helpful to a particular analysis.

Paragraphs: These are rarely used, because many paragraphs are often not synonymous and are hard to quantify as patterns or threads of common research.

Items: In that an item may represent a letter, a speech, a section, a diary entry, or even an in-depth interview, items are very helpful.

Concepts: These are a more sophisticated type of word counting. For example, the concept of deviance may have word clusters that are associated with it, such as crime, delinquency, and fraud.

Semantics: Researchers are often interested in more than the type of word being used; rather, a focus in semantic counting often shifts to the strength or weakness of a word.

Figure 9.2. Stage Model of Qualitative Content Analysis

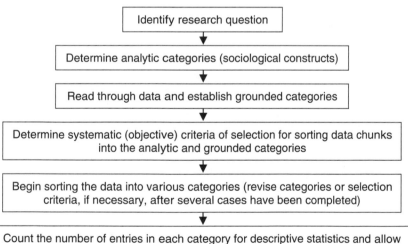

CONTENT REVIEW

1. What guidelines for information collection and interpretation are followed by case study researchers?
2. Think of a situation in which you create dozens of pages of field notes and several interview transcriptions but fail to properly label and store this information. What problems related to information interpretation might you experience?

ACTIVITIES AND APPLICATIONS FOR PROSPECTIVE RESEARCHERS

1. Find a dissertation using case study research and describe the various sources of information. What methods of information collection and interpretation are used by the researcher?
2. Interview a university researcher and describe that person's system for information collection and interpretation.
3. Which information collection and interpretation guidelines are most appropriate to your case study research? How do you intend to abide by those guidelines? Which guideline may be the most difficult to follow?

CHAPTER 10

Reporting Findings

A case study researcher synthesizes the many disparate pieces of information acquired during the research process in order to identify and report meaningful findings. Researchers have developed several strategies (e.g., thematic analysis, categorical analysis, narrative analysis) for accomplishing this task, largely related to the disciplinary orientation and design used to guide the case study. Although each strategy has unique characteristics, most strategies have in common a basic process—repetitive, ongoing review of accumulated information in order to identify recurrent patterns, themes, or categories. Thematic analysis is often preferred by novice researchers. Through use of this strategy, each new piece of information is examined in light of a particular research question in order to construct a tentative answer to the question. Tentative answers are categorized into themes. This process continues until themes emerge that are well supported by all available information. During this process, the case study researcher may elect to refine the question if the information is disconfirming or retain the question if the information supports the question's viability. Once information from all sources is thoroughly reviewed, themes for which the preponderance of information supports a tentative answer are retained and reported as findings.

Determination of information-supported themes that address the research questions is a critical endeavor of a case study researcher. Several criteria exist by which to judge the extent to which a researcher's themes accurately and comprehensively represent the information collected in the study. First, the themes must reflect the purpose of the research and respond to the questions under investigation. Second, the themes must evolve from a saturation of the collected information. In other words, in his or her creation of themes, the researcher must exhaust all information gathered in the study that is relevant to the research questions. Third, although themes are sometimes hierarchical and interconnected, novice researchers should seek to develop themes that represent separate and distinct categories of findings. Overlapping or contradictory themes often suggest the need for additional synthesis of the findings. Fourth, each theme should be as specific and explanatory as is allowed by the data. For example, the theme "Administrators favor computer software programs that are available and inexpensive, but not necessarily efficient," is more specific and explanatory than the theme "Administrators use invalid criteria when they adopt computer software programs." Finally, themes should be of comparable complexity. An example of comparably complex themes created by a teacher exploring student attrition at her school may be "Many students drop out of school because of their dissatisfaction with teachers who routinely lecture" and "Many students quit school to work in order to earn discretionary money."

Although there is no universally accepted format for writing a case study research report, certain components are commonly found in most reports. As a minimum, the report should articulate the event, situation, program, or activity under investigation, and how the research effort is bounded by time and space. The researcher should explain his or her relationship to that being researched and any personal biases brought to the setting. The research report should reflect the literature related to the topic under investigation and how that literature informs the research questions. Some factors that must be addressed are the disciplinary orientation and research design of the study and how they influence the information-gathering strategies used in the study. Details related to all information collection strategies, to include interviews, observations, and document reviews should be explained. The report should be richly descriptive and include key participants' statements that elucidate significant findings. Finally, the strategies used to interpret, report, and confirm the case study's findings should be articulated.

The primary characteristic of reporting findings when doing case study research is repetitive, continual review of obtained information to identify answers to questions being investigated. The process is generally facilitated by categorizing information into themes that represent tentative and then final outcomes for the research. Identifying themes involves a series of steps that end in a collection of parallel findings representing the results of the investigation. Reports of case study research reflect all aspects of the investigative process using integrated sections of text or illustrative tables to reduce the typical volumes of available information to meaningful units for confirmation and dissemination.

HOW TO SYNTHESIZE FINDINGS

Case studies generate large amounts of information from different sources. Synthesizing this information means combining, integrating, and summarizing findings. Answering the following questions may facilitate the process of synthesizing information:

- What information from different sources goes together?
- Within a source, what information can be grouped?
- What arguments contribute to grouping information together?
- What entities bounded by space and time are shared?
- How do various sources of information affect findings?
- What information links various findings together?
- What previous work provides a basis for analysis?
- What questions are being answered?
- What generalizations can be made?

Case study findings can also be synthesized and presented based on the sources that provide the information. Commonly used information sources and examples are shown in Table 10.1.

Table 10.1. Information Sources Used in Case Study Research

Information Source	*Examples*
People	• Individuals, groups
Places	• Schools, playgrounds
Things	• Artifacts, objects
Events	• Football game, worship service
Organizations	• American Medical Association, Association of Teacher Educators
Documents	• Progress reports, annual evaluations

DESIGN ILLUSTRATION

(Critique Checklist for a Case Study Report. Adapted from R. Stake. [1995]. *The art of case study research*. Thousand Oaks, CA: Sage.)

These criteria may help you define, assess, and write a case study report:

- Is the text easy to read and understand?
- Does it fit together with sentences building to paragraphs that convey overall meaning as a whole?

- Does the report have a conceptual structure evident in headings that are used to organize the content (i.e., themes or issues)?
- Are concerns, issues, or problems developed in a serious and scholarly way?
- Is the case defined clearly so others can generalize from it, replicate it, or both?
- Is there a sense of story to the presentation?
- Is the reader provided some vicarious experience?
- Have quotations been used effectively, not overly extensively?
- Are headings, figures, artifacts, appendixes, and indexes used effectively?
- Is there evidence that the report was carefully edited?
- Has the writer made sound assertions, neither over- nor under-generalizing or interpreting findings?
- Has adequate attention been paid to various key aspects of the work?
- Was sufficient information presented to justify confidence in findings and conclusions?
- Were information sources well chosen and sufficient in number, scope, and content?
- Were multiple information sources used as a basis for outcomes?
- Is the role and point of view of the researcher evident?
- Is the nature of the audience evident?
- Is the reporting sensitive to multiple perspectives?

CONTENT REVIEW

1. What basic processes are used by case study researchers to report their findings?
2. What are the criteria used to determine the extent to which a researcher's themes accurately and comprehensively represent the information collected in the study?
3. What components are typically found in a case study research report?

ACTIVITIES AND APPLICATIONS FOR
PROSPECTIVE RESEARCHERS

1. Find a dissertation using case study research and describe how the results were reported.

2. Find a journal article that describes case study research and answer the Critique Checklist for a Case Study Report (see above).
3. What themes have emerged from your case study research? How were they derived? Which processes for reporting findings did you implement? How do you intend to report your study's findings?

CHAPTER 11

Confirming Case Study Findings

Once all information is gathered, synthesized, and reported, a case study researcher should confirm the findings of the study before disseminating a final report. Several strategies exist through which to confirm one's findings. A case study researcher should implement as many of these strategies as is possible.

Perhaps the most powerful strategy to confirm a report's findings is to share the results with those examined in the study. This activity extends the intent of the researcher's ethical obligation to debrief participants in the study. The goal of gaining feedback from those studied is to gather their perceptions of the plausibility of the findings based on the information that the participants themselves provided.

Another strategy involves review of the report by fellow case study researchers who are familiar with the goals and procedures of case study research. These colleagues should systematically and thoroughly critique the study's procedures and findings in order to identify discrepancies that may threaten the credibility of the research effort.

A related strategy is to solicit scrutiny of the final report from experts on the topic under investigation. For example, a teacher exploring student attrition at her school may ask fellow teachers outside the setting of the case study to analyze her report for accuracy, clarity, and meaningfulness.

A fourth strategy involves the researcher's articulation of personal biases brought to the situation and how he or she attempted to mitigate the potential effects of those biases. Acknowledgment of one's biases combined with an explanation of how the researcher prevented those biases from influencing the research process and findings lessens the likelihood that the researcher will be accused of producing contrived findings.

A fifth strategy for confirming results is to demonstrate how findings are based on information acquired from multiple sources, sometimes called *triangulation*. Findings based on evidence attained from interviews, observations, and documents are more convincing than those based on evidence from only one or two of these information sources. Similarly, like most researchers, those doing case study research typically relate their findings to the work of others.

Case study researchers verify and confirm their findings before offering them for widespread dissemination, review, and reaction. They accomplish this by sharing the outcomes of their work with participants, with their colleagues, or with experts on the topic that was studied. They also disclose their personal biases regarding the topic and delimit how they controlled them when conducting the investigation. They use multiple methods to identify their findings. Like researchers reporting findings from studies that used other methodologies, case study researchers generally relate their findings to the work of others as another method of confirming and building confidence in what was discovered as a result of the study.

ILLUSTRATIONS FROM PRACTICE

Illustration 1

While conducting a case study involving a teacher, Stake (1995) prepared a draft report of his findings that he believed included an accurate portrayal of the teacher's actions and words. Implementing the process called "member checking," Stake asked the teacher to examine the draft report for accuracy and palatability. On this occasion, the teacher found the report objectionable and embarrassing. As a result, Stake revised the report.

Illustration 2

Upon completion of a case study research effort, a summary form may help researchers and participants confirm findings and preserve a record of events. An example of a summary form follows.

- Title of project
- Time period of research
- Date of ethics approval
- Identification of researchers
- Literature used to provide background and justification for research
- Description of research hypotheses
- Sample or population studied
- Explanation of all information collection procedures
- Findings
- Interpretation of findings
- Conclusions and recommendations based on findings

- Problems encountered during research
- Limitations of research
- Dissemination of results

CONTENT REVIEW

1. What strategies are commonly used by case study researchers to confirm findings?
2. How does attaining information from multiple sources help to confirm the results of a case study research effort?

ACTIVITIES AND APPLICATIONS FOR
PROSPECTIVE RESEARCHERS

1. Find a journal article that involves case study research and describe how the findings of the study are confirmed.
2. Suppose a school administrator is conducting research on causes of teacher absenteeism at her school. She asks you how she may increase the probability that her case study research report will be accepted as credible. What advice would you provide her?
3. What are your personal biases that may influence your case study research project? How are you addressing those biases? What other strategies for confirming your study's findings are you implementing?

PART III

Putting It All Together

CHAPTER 12

Preparing Proposals for Case Study Research

A proposal is a formal document advancing an original point of view supported by research. In general, the purpose of a research proposal is to establish the context for a study, to demonstrate the need for a study, to illustrate how the study will address the need using appropriate research methods, and to provide assurances that participation will not harm participants. Before proceeding with a full-scale research effort, novice researchers must often submit proposals that allow more experienced researchers to see how the novice researchers might communicate the rationale and content for a study to an interested audience. At many universities, proposals are used to justify and gain approval for research to be completed by graduate students enrolled in advanced-degree programs.

Although proposals vary in content and scope, they often contain three chapters—introduction, review of literature, and method—and supporting materials.

INTRODUCTION

The first chapter usually begins with an overview of the research problem. The researcher provides a natural progression of ideas and constructs that culminates with the purpose of the study. This section is followed by a description of the delimitations and limitations of the study and any assumptions or unique definitions that describe, clarify, or elaborate the work that will be done. *Delimitations* are the boundaries of research as it is being proposed and include such information as the "case" being investigated and a brief description of its characteristics. *Limitations* are factors that may affect the results of the study and that are generally beyond the control of the researcher. *Assumptions* are preliminary beliefs that are made about the study in general. This section of Chapter 1 places the research into a context that supports confidence in the likelihood that it will be completed as planned and will provide answers to the questions under investigation. Definitions of formal terms or constructs central to the research are included before a brief section in which the researcher summarizes the key aspects of the study that have been presented in this first chapter.

REVIEW OF LITERATURE

The second chapter usually begins with a paragraph in which the researcher describes the contents of the review of literature (e.g., *theoretical basis* or *framework* for the study, the *conceptual foundations* for the research, the *summative knowledge base*). The chapter is usually divided into labeled subsections illustrating the broad topics being addressed. It ends with a summary of the knowledge base that serves as justification for the study.

METHOD

The method chapter of the proposal includes a brief description of the contents. This is followed by sections addressing preliminary or pilot-study work, if appropriate. The bulk of this chapter involves descriptions of the expected participants, settings, and planned procedures, including methods for information collection and planned analyses. It concludes with a brief summary.

Case study research methods allow researchers to capture multiple realities that are not easily quantifiable. This approach differs from those of other methods in its holistic approach to information collection in natural settings and its use of purposive sampling techniques. Here is how the "method" in a case study research proposal might be summarized (see Lehmann, 1998):

> The researcher will conduct open-ended interviews with single parents in order to listen to their unique points of view and to examine parenthood from their unique perspective. Each participant will be interviewed once for approximately 90 minutes. Interviews will be tape-recorded and then transcribed in order to categorize information into a coding scheme. The transcript

lengths will likely range 20 to 30 pages resulting in the analysis of a comprehensive set of interview information. An inductive, iterative process of reading and rereading the transcriptions will be used to produce subcategories for information analysis within the context of three research areas of interest: (a) fathers' perspectives and roles, (b) mothers' perspectives and roles, and (c) differences in perspectives between the two types of single parents. Statements will be partitioned into units, grouped in common category headings, analyzed, and summarized. Plausibility of subcategories will be established by testing them with new information units until all relevant information has been assigned to a category. In this way, common codes will be identified and differences between participants noted. Establishing information analysis credibility will also involve (a) implementing interrater reliability coding checks, (b) uncovering biases that might skew the researcher's perspective, and (c) comparing obtained outcomes to previously published research findings.

SUPPORTING MATERIALS

References, appendixes, and human subjects' assurances are typically included as the final parts of a research proposal. You should include in the reference list *only* those sources and *all* the sources *cited* in the proposal. This is different from a more general bibliography that reflects a list of sources used in your research. For example, you might use this book in developing your proposal, but you would not need to include it in the references unless you provided a specific citation for it related to some aspect of your study. Think of the references as "works cited" in the proposal, not all the sources that could have been used to develop it. Include in separate appendixes copies of instruments, interview protocols, information collection forms and programs, or written information that you plan to use in your study. Because all research that involves humans *must* be reviewed and approved by the appropriate research ethics committees, most proposals for research in graduate programs include information related to the approval process, which sometimes requires preparation of a separate, brief description of your research. When the proposal has been approved by the appropriate committee(s), the study may commence.

FREQUENTLY ASKED QUESTIONS ABOUT
RESEARCH PROPOSALS

Chapter 1

1. Is there a simple way to think about what is included in Chapter 1?

The best way to "introduce" your study is by addressing a few key questions:

- What is the goal of the research or the problem to be addressed?
- Why is the goal or solving the problem important?
- What do we already know about it?
- What do we need to know in order to advance knowledge, achieve the goal, or solve the problem?
- How do you plan to achieve the goal or solve the problem?

Your job is to convince the reader that you will be addressing an important problem that needs to be addressed in the manner that you have chosen.

2. What do I "define" in my section on "definition of terms?" How can I connect my definitions with the relevance of the study? I defined the terms so that people would have more information about them (example: definition of what an urban school is). I am not sure what you are looking for.

Usually the definitions are reserved for special terms that are unique to the study being conducted. They are formal, operational descriptions of constructs central to the research. In the case of *an urban school* (or any other term), you would only need to define it if your definition was different, for some reason, from the one that most people would already know or if it represented a special term that most people would be unfamiliar with in their daily lives (e.g., *North Carolina ABCs* require a definition because the term refers to something different from what most people associate with *ABCs*).

3. Is an assumptions section necessary and what needs to be incorporated in this area?

A section on assumptions is not necessary. Assumptions are preliminary (i.e., before the study begins) beliefs that are made about the parameters of the study in general or about the case being studied, the instruments, or other aspects of the work. This section puts the research into a context that supports confidence in the likelihood it will be completed as planned and will provide answers to questions under investigation. For example, we might assume that a survey is the best method for information collection because much of the previous research in that area was completed using surveys. Or we might include students, parents, and teachers in our drop-out-rate study because we assume that including one without the others will be inadequate based on what is known about why students fail to finish school.

4. Do you always have limitations and delimitations? Do you have one or the other or both? I have seen so many different dissertations and the setup is always different.

You can include one, the other, or both depending on what aspect of your research you are "introducing" to the reader. Delimitations are the parameters of a study and include such information as the individuals being studied and a brief description of their characteristics. This section describes the group to which generalizations can be safely made. Delimitations define what the researcher has decided to do (e.g., use these people for these reasons). Limitations are factors that may affect the results of the study and are generally beyond the control of the researcher. This section describes the limiting conditions or restrictive weaknesses of the study. These factors are sometimes revealed after the study has been completed.

Chapter 2

1. Is there a simple way to think about what is included in Chapter 2?

The best way to "make the case" for your study is by addressing a few key questions:

- What is the goal of the research or the problem to be addressed? (This is a restatement from Chapter 1.) For example:

Large numbers of professionals leave the teaching field each year; the goal of this research is the implementation and evaluation of a program designed to improve the retention of classroom teachers.

- Why is the goal or solving the problem important? (Again, a restatement from Chapter 1.) For example:

Teacher shortages are at the highest rates in history; the social, economic, and educational costs of teachers leaving before retirement are very high; and the need for programs designed to reduce these shortages is clear.

- What do we know?
- What is known about the broad underlying context for the study?
- What do we know about teacher shortages and supply and demand in teaching?
- What do we know about the costs of teacher attrition?
- What do we know about factors that influence teacher attrition?
- What is known about the specific context for the study?
- What do we know about programs that help retain classroom teachers and reduce attrition?
- What do we need to know to advance knowledge, achieve the goal, or solve the problem?
- How do you plan to achieve the goal or solve the problem?

Your job is to convince the reader that you will be addressing an important problem that needs to be addressed.

2. Where do I start?

The best way to start a literature review is by stating the "problem" that will be addressed. Consider the following: Discipline is a continuing concern in America's schools. While models of discipline have been studied, effectiveness has largely been documented using perceptions of teachers and other professionals. Few studies have documented changes in classroom behaviors of teachers and/or students that result from the application of systematic discipline programs. The purpose of this research is . . .

3. Why am I including a review of literature in a research proposal? Should I not be focusing on the method?

The literature review establishes the need for the study. It provides a clear illustration of what is known and what needs to be known about a topic.

4. How do I end a literature review?

All parts of the literature point to a final summary statement of the problem and how it will be addressed. Using a table is a good way to summarize the key findings from the literature review. If you use a table, be sure to describe it in the text so that it does not stand alone in the chapter. The message of a literature review is an integrated analysis of what is known and not known about an important problem; the focus of the final section of Chapter 2 is an integrated summary of the literature review.

Chapter 3

1. Is there a simple way to think about what is included in Chapter 3?

Chapter 3 is best represented as a technical map for what the researcher is proposing. It usually includes a description of the "participant(s)" who will provide information that will be used to answer the research question(s). How the information will be gathered (i.e., the "procedures") and analyzed is also part of the method chapter. After this chapter is written, there should be no doubt about what will be happening when the study is implemented.

2. Where do I start?

The best way to start a discussion of the method is by restating the "problem" that will be addressed. This is the same problem that was introduced in Chapter 1 and "justified" in Chapter 2. By beginning Chapter 3 with a restatement of the problem, the researcher provides a logical link among the key parts of the proposal.

CONTENT REVIEW

1. What chapters are generally included in most case study research proposals? What is normally included in the first chapter? Second chapter? Third chapter?
2. What types of supporting materials are found in case study research proposals?

ACTIVITIES AND APPLICATIONS FOR PROSPECTIVE RESEARCHERS

1. How might a proposal to conduct case study research differ from a proposal to conduct a survey of public attitudes toward the nation's health-care system?
2. Considering your own case study research project, what would be the first step in developing a proposal to justify and gain approval for the research to be completed as a final requirement in a graduate program? What would you include in the first, second, and third chapters of your proposal?

CHAPTER 13

Disseminating Case Study Research

To allow others to benefit from the research, case study researchers disseminate their findings in many ways. Two common means of doing so are through communications with colleagues and other stakeholders at professional conferences and through publication in scholarly journals. Preparing a formal report of the outcomes of a case study research effort is similar to preparing a proposal to conduct the study. The main difference is that reports presented at conferences or published in journals also include a thorough presentation of the study's findings and a discussion of what the findings mean. Because formal report writing for publication in scholarly journals is a particularly daunting task for many novice researchers, we offer several suggestions in this chapter.

Writers of case study research reports that are submitted for publication should pay particular attention to the expectations of the journal and its editors. Most studies in a particular professional journal are presented in a similar format; therefore, a sound way to prepare a manuscript for submission to a particular journal is to review the style of the journal's articles and then model that style in your own writing.

Typically, articles published in journals include an *introduction*, a section describing the *method*, the study's *results* (possibly supplemented with tables or figures), a *discussion of what it all means* (with emphasis on linking the work to extant literature), and a presentation of *implications* of the work for improving the knowledge base and professional practice (see Algozzine, Spooner, & Karvonen, 2002). Of course, the content, emphasis, and length of each section will vary with the thrust of the article, the audience, and the nature of the study. The following sections provide information often found in published articles that may help you publish your case study research.

INTRODUCTION

The introduction to the article makes the purpose, worth, and need for the research immediately clear; that is, it describes what is known about the topic under investigation, why the study was necessary, what was intended to be accomplished, and why the outcomes are important. The introduction is usually not labeled as such but normally includes a succinct review of literature that directs the need, purpose, and importance of the study. A good introduction gives the reader a clear sense of what was done and why (see American Psychological Association [APA], 2001, p. 16). A number of questions are addressed:

- What is the point of the study?
- How do the questions and design relate to the problem?
- What are the theoretical implications of the work and how does the work relate to previous research in the area?
- What are the theoretical propositions tested and how were they arrived at?

METHOD

The method section describes in detail how the study was conducted (see APA, 2001, pp. 17–20). Begin with an overview of the method that was used to conduct the study. A list of questions or a sentence outlining the purpose and objectives can also be used to introduce the method before a formal description of what was done in the study is provided. This description should provide the reader with sufficient information to evaluate the appropriateness and integrity of what was done as well as the credibility of the outcomes derived from doing it. The goal here is to provide essential information that allows others to comprehend the study. Whereas insufficient detail leaves the reader with questions, too much detail burdens the reader with irrelevant information.

RESULTS

The results section summarizes the information collected and how it is used to address the case study's research questions (see APA, 2001, pp. 20–26). The main outcomes are typically presented first, with sufficient detail to justify conclusions with regard to primary and secondary questions. All relevant results, predicted ones as well as those that were not expected, should be addressed, including those that run counter to preconceived questions. Case study results vary widely according to the information collected and the analysis method used; as a result, there is generally great flexibility in the manner in which they are reported (see McWilliam, 2000). Nevertheless, the results section should include the identification of common or emergent themes, exceptions to the primary findings, and unexpected outcomes. Most findings are reported within the text and may be supported with direct quotes from participants or examples that support the findings. However, some information may be best reported or summarized graphically in tables or figures.

Most journals rarely have space for more than two or three tables or figures in an article. Before you include a table or figure, try to decide if it contains vital information that helps to organize the presentation of findings. Use tables to provide exact values and efficiently illustrate outcomes. Use figures, such as charts and pictures, to illustrate outcomes that are not as precise as those presented in tables (e.g., an ethnographic-decision model that cannot be adequately conveyed in tabular form). Summarizing outcomes in tables and figures instead of in the text can be very helpful, especially when large amounts of information are reduced by representation in a form other than sentences in paragraphs; however, using tables or figures for information that can easily be presented in a few sentences of text is not a good idea. Tables and figures should augment rather than duplicate text, conveying essential facts without adding distracting details. The goal is to achieve a parsimonious balance in presenting the outcomes of the study. If you use tables and figures, mention them in the text. Refer to all tables as *tables* and all charts, graphs, photographs, drawings, or other depictions as *figures*. Tables and figures supplement the text; they do not stand alone. Always tell the reader what to look for in the tables and figures and provide sufficient explanation to make the presentation easily comprehensible (see APA, 2001, pp. 147–201).

DISCUSSION

The discussion section ties the outcomes of the research to the literature and takes readers beyond the facts to the meaning they reflect, to the questions they raise, to the ideas to which they point, and to the practical uses and value they have for the extension of knowledge. Consider opening the discussion with a clear statement relating the findings to the original research questions. Similarities and differences between the study's outcomes and those of the work of others are also useful beginnings for the final section of the article. Be careful, however, not to simply refor-mulate, rehash, and repeat points made earlier in the article. Statements in the discussion should contribute to a position and the reader's under-standing of the issue being researched. Finally, do not overemphasize limitations and do not generalize beyond the outcomes of the study. Speculation is in order only if it is (a) identified as such, (b) related closely and logically to the information collected or theory discussed in the study, and (c) expressed concisely (APA, 1994, p. 19).

CONTENT REVIEW

1. What are the main sections typically included in a manuscript submitted for publication based on case study research?
2. What are the primary factors to consider when writing the results and discussion sections of a case study research report?

ACTIVITIES AND APPLICATIONS FOR PROSPECTIVE RESEARCHERS

1. What are some ways in which you may disseminate information about the outcomes of case study research?
2. How might you outline, for submission to a professional journal, a manuscript of a case study research effort on gang violence in inner cities?
3. What key components would you need to include if you prepared your case study research project for publication?

Epilogue

All research involves finding answers to questions that an individual investigator or a team of researchers believes are important. Decisions about the quality of the research are determined by the way in which it is conducted, not the type of research used to generate the answers. The steps we describe in this book represent one useful set of questions to address when doing case study research. Table E.1 lists each step and its corresponding questions.

We hope that our work has encouraged you to do case study research. If it has, we would be honored if you would share your research with us.

Dawson Hancock

Bob Algozzine

Educational Leadership

The University of North Carolina at Charlotte

Charlotte, North Carolina 28223-0001

704-687-8858

704-687-3493(FAX)

DHancock@email.uncc.edu

Table E.1. Sequence of Procedures in Case Study Research

Step	Activity	Questions to Address
1.	Setting the Stage	• What are you going to study? • Why is case study research appropriate for your research?
2.	Determining What We Know	• What do we already know about what you are going to study? • What do we need to know about it? • Has a previous case study been completed addressing the same or similar questions as in your research? • What other types of research have been used to answer questions similar to those in your research?
3.	Selecting a Design	• Are you interested in exploring patterns of behavior, describing past or current conditions, describing characteristics or behaviors of specific individuals, or describing broad aspects of society? • Are you interested in describing individual cases, explaining theories, or extending an extant knowledge base?
4.	Getting Information from Interviews	• Can what you need to know be obtained by asking other people questions? • Have other researchers addressed similar questions using interviews?
5.	Getting Information from Observations	• Can what you need to know be obtained by watching other people? • Have other researchers addressed similar questions using observations?
6.	Getting Information from Documents	• Can what you need to know be obtained by reviewing materials, records, or other similar information? • Have other researchers addressed similar questions using existing documents?
7.	Summarizing and Interpreting Information	• How will the information that is gathered be reduced to reflect answers to questions being investigated? • How will the outcomes of your research be linked to the work of others?
8.	Reporting Findings	• How will the information that is gathered be reduced to reflect answers to questions being investigated? • What is the simplest form for sharing the outcomes of your research with others?
9.	Confirming Findings	• What approach will be taken to establish confidence in the findings of your research? • What do participants in your research or experts in the field think of the outcomes of your research? • To what extent are the outcomes of your research linked to the findings of others? • Have other researchers reported similar answers to questions like those investigated in your research?

Key Terms

bias: a preference or an inclination, especially one that inhibits impartial judgment

case study: a detailed analysis of a person or group, especially as a model of medical, psychiatric, psychological, or social phenomena

collective case study: a project that attempts to address an issue in question while adding to the literature base that helps conceptualize a theory

dissertation: a lengthy, formal treatise, especially one written by a candidate for the doctoral degree at a university; a thesis

external auditor: one who has no known connection to a study so that he or she may examine its procedures as supported by the information

ethnographic case study: a work that deals with the scientific description of specific human cultures

historical case study: a work that deals with descriptions of events, programs, or organizations as they have evolved over time

hypothesis: a proposed explanation that is offered for an observation, phenomenon, or scientific problem and that can be tested by further investigation

interview: a conversation, such as one conducted by a researcher, in which facts or statements are elicited from a subject

interview guide: five to six open-ended questions that the interviewer will ask the interviewee

instrumental case study: a work of which the purpose is to gain a better understanding of a theoretical question or problem

intrinsic case study: a work that has as its focus to learn more about a particular individual, group, event, or organization instead of generalizing broad-based research findings

literature review: an account of what has been published on a topic by accredited scholars and researchers

member check: the act of taking information back to the participants so that they can judge the accuracy or credibility of the account

observation: the act of noting and recording something, such as a phenomenon, with instruments

observation guide: a list of features to be addressed during a particular observation

peer reviewer: one who keeps the researcher honest and asks difficult questions regarding the research

phenomenon: a particular event, situation, program, or activity to be observed

private records: materials produced by an individual that provide insight into that person's beliefs, attitudes, and behaviors

psychological case study: a work that is grounded in personal experiences and ways of looking at the world

public records: documents that reflect beliefs, attitudes, and behaviors beyond those of an individual

qualitative research: any kind of research that produces findings not arrived at through statistical procedures or other means of quantification

quantitative research: investigation that seeks causal determination, prediction, and generalization of findings arrived at via statistical measures

recursive: an expression where each term of which is determined by application of a formula to preceding terms

reliability: a factor yielding the same or compatible results in different clinical experiments or statistical trials

research design: the element used to structure the research, to show how all the major parts of the research project—the samples or groups, measures, treatments, or programs and methods of assignment—are designed to address the central research questions

sociological case study: a work grounded in the structure, development, interaction, and collective behavior of groups or individuals

survey: an overview that encompasses any measurement procedures that involve asking questions of respondents; can be anything from a short paper-and-pencil feedback form to an intensive one-on-one in-depth interview

triangulation: the application and combination of several research methodologies in the study of the same phenomenon

transcript: a record of verbal communication, especially a written, typewritten, or printed copy

References

Abramson, P. R. (1992). *A case for case studies*. Thousand Oaks, CA: Sage.

Adler, P. A., & Adler, P. (1991). *Backboards and blackboards: College athletes and role engulfment*. New York: Columbia.

Algozzine, B., Spooner, F., & Karvonen, M. (2002). *How to prepare a research article in APA style*. Arlington, VA: Council for Exceptional Children.

American Psychological Association. (1994). *Publication manual of the American Psychological Association* (4th ed.). Washington, DC: Author.

American Psychological Association. (2001). *Publication manual of the American Psychological Association* (5th ed.). Washington, DC: Author.

Asmussen, K. J., & Creswell, J. W. (1995). Campus response to a student gunman. *Journal of Higher Education, 66*(5), 575–591.

Benton-Kupper, J. (1999). Can less be more? The quantity versus quality issue of curriculum in a block schedule. *Journal of Research and Development in Education, 32*(3), 168–177.

Berg, B. L. (2004). *Qualitative research methods for the social sciences* (5th ed.). New York: Pearson Education.

Bloom, B. S. (1984). *Taxonomy of educational objectives*. Boston: Pearson.

Bogden, R. C., & Bilken, S. K. (2003). *Qualitative research in education: An introduction to theories and methods* (4th ed.). New York: Allyn and Bacon.

Bond, L. B., Jaeger, R., Smith, T., & Hattie, J. (2001). Defrocking the National Board: The certification system of the National Board for Professional Teaching Standards. *Education Matters, 1*(2), 79–82.

Clark, G. K. (1967). *The critical historian*. Portsmouth, NH: Heinemann Educational Books.

Creswell, J. W. (1998). *Qualitative inquiry and research design: Choosing among five traditions*. Thousand Oaks, CA: Sage.

Creswell, J. W. (2005). *Educational research: Planning, conducting, and evaluating quantitative and qualitative research* (2nd ed.). Upper Saddle River, NJ: Prentice Hall.

Crudden, A. (2002). Employment after vision loss: Results of a collective case study. *Journal of Visual Impairment and Blindness, 96*(9), 615–621.

D'Emidio-Caston, M., & Brown, J. H. (1998). The other side of the story: Student narratives on the California Drug, Alcohol, and Tobacco Education programs. *Evaluation Review, 22*(1), 95–117.

Ely, M., Anzul, M., Friedman, T., Garner, D., & Steinmetz, A. C. (1991). *Doing qualitative research: Circles within circles*. New York: Falmer.

Erlandson, D. A., Harris, E. L., Skipper, B. L., & Allen, S. D. (1993). *Doing naturalistic inquiry: A guide to methods.* Newbury Park, CA: Sage.

Flinders, D. J., & Mills, G. E. (1993). *Theory and concepts in qualitative research.* New York: Teachers College Press.

Galvan, J. L. (1999). *Writing literature reviews: A guide for students of social and behavioral sciences.* Los Angeles: Pyrczak.

Gardner, H. (1999). *Intelligence reframed: Multiple intelligences for the 21st century.* New York: Basic Books.

Glesne, C., & Peshkin, A. (1992). *Becoming qualitative researchers: An introduction.* White Plains, NY: Longman.

Hatch, J. A. (2002). *Doing qualitative research in education settings.* Albany: State University of New York Press.

Hook, D. (2003). Reading Geldenhuys: Constructing and deconstructing the Norwood killer. *South African Journal of Psychology, 33*(1), 1–9.

Horn, E., Lieber, J., Li, S., Sandall, S., & Schwartz, I. (2000). Supporting young children's IEP goals in inclusive settings through embedded learning opportunities. *Topics in Early Childhood Education, 20*(4), 208–224.

Howe, K., Eisenhart, M., & Betebenner, D. (2002). The price of public school choice. *Educational Leadership, 59*(7), 20–25.

Hughes, M. (1998). Turning points in the lives of young inner-city men forgoing destructive criminal behaviors: A qualitative study. *Social Work Research, 22*(3), 143–151.

Kalnins, Z. G. (1986). *An exploratory study of the meaning of life as described by residents of a long-term care facility.* Project proposal, Peabody College of Vanderbilt University, Nashville, TN.

Kincannon, J. M. (2002). *From the classroom to the Web: A study of faculty change.* Paper presented at the meeting of the American Educational Research Association, New Orleans, LA. (ERIC Document Reproduction Service No. ED467096)

Ladany, N., O'Brien, K. M., Hill, C. E., Melincoff, D. S., Knox, S., & Peterson, D. A. (1997). Sexual attraction toward clients, use of supervision, and prior training: A qualitative study of pre-doctoral psychology interns. *Journal of Counseling Psychology, 44*(4), 413–424.

Lancy, D. F. (1993). *Qualitative research in education: An introduction to the major traditions.* White Plains, New York: Longman.

Lankard, A., & McLaughlin, W. J. (2003). Marketing an environmental issue: A case study of the Wilderness Society's core messages to promote national forest conversation from 1964 to 2000. *Society and Natural Resources, 16*(5), 415–434.

Lecompte, M. D., & Preissle, J. (1993). *Ethnography and qualitative design in educational research.* (2nd ed.). Orlando, FL: Academic Press.

Lehmann, J. P. (1998). Mothers' roles: A comparison between mothers of adolescents with severe disabilities and mothers of vocational students. *Career Development for Exceptional Individuals, 21*(2), 129–143.

Lincoln, Y. S., & Guba, E. G. (1985). *Naturalistic inquiry.* Beverly Hills, CA: Sage.

Marshall, C. (1981). Organizational policy and women's socialization in administration. *Urban Education, 16*(2), 205–231.

Marshall, C., & Rossman, G. B. (1999). *Designing qualitative research* (3rd ed.). Thousand Oaks, CA: Sage.

Mason, J. (2002). *Qualitative researching* (2nd ed.). Thousand Oaks, CA: Sage.

McWilliam, R. A. (2000). Reporting qualitative studies. *Journal of Early Intervention, 23*(2), 77–80.

Merriam, S. B. (1998). *Case study research in education: A qualitative approach.* San Francisco: Jossey-Bass.

Merriam, S. B. (2001). *Qualitative research and case study applications in education.* San Francisco: Jossey-Bass.

Miles, M. B., & Huberman, A. M. (1994). *Qualitative information analysis: A sourcebook of new methods* (2nd ed.). Thousand Oaks, CA: Sage.

Mueller, A., & Fleming, T. (2001). Cooperative learning: Listening to how children work at school. *Journal of Educational Research, 94*(5), 259–366.

Patton, M. Q. (1980). *Qualitative evaluation methods.* Beverly Hills, CA: Sage.

Patton, M. Q. (1990). *Qualitative evaluation and research methods* (2nd ed.). Newbury Park, CA: Sage.

Patton, M. Q. (2002). *Qualitative research and evaluation methods* (3rd ed.). Newbury Park, CA: Sage.

Place, A. W., & Wood, G. S. (1999). A case study of traditionally underrepresented individuals' experiences in a doctoral program. *Journal for a Just and Caring Education, 5*(4), 442–456.

Rhoads, R. A. (1998). In the service of citizenship: A study of student involvement in community service. *The Journal of Higher Education, 69*(3), 277–297.

Rossman, G. B. (1985, April). *Studying professional cultures in improving high schools.* Paper presented at the annual meeting of the American Educational Research Association, Chicago.

Rossman, G. B., Corbett, H. D., & Firestone, W. A. (1984). *Plan for the study of professional cultures in improving high schools.* Philadelphia: Research for Better Schools.

Salamon, S. (2003). From hometown to nontown: Rural community effects to suburbanization. *Rural Sociology, 68*(1), 1–24.

Seidman, I. (2006*). Interviewing as qualitative research: A guide for researchers in education and the social sciences* (3rd ed.). New York: Teachers College Press.

Stake, R. (1995). *The art of case study research.* Thousand Oaks, CA: Sage.

Stine, D. E. (1998). *A change in administration: A significant organizational life event* (Report No. EA029296). Educational Management. (ERIC Document Reproduction Service No. ED425509).

Thomas, W. I., & Znaniecki, F. (1927). *The Polish peasant in Europe and America.* New York: Knopf.

Thorne, B. (1993). Political activists as participant observer: Conflicts of commitment in a study of the draft resistance movement of the 1960s. In R. Emerson (Ed.), *Contemporary field research: A collection of readings* (pp. 216–234). Prospect Heights, IL: Waveland.

Utsey, S. O., Howard, A., & Williams, O. (2003). Therapeutic group mentoring with African American male adolescents. *Journal of Mental Health Counseling, 25*(2), 126–139.

Wolcott, H. F. (1973). *The man in the principal's office: An ethnography.* Austin, TX: Holt, Rinehart and Winston.

Yin, R. K. (1994). *Case study research: Design and methods* (2nd ed.). Thousand Oaks, CA: Sage.

Yin, R. K. (2003). *Case study research: Design and methods* (3rd ed.). Thousand Oaks, CA: Sage.

Annotated Bibliography

The following is a list of books that address at least one aspect of doing case study research; each citation is followed by a brief paragraph (i.e., the annotation) prepared to provide additional information (e.g., author's point of view, representativeness of case study research in the content) about the sources. We followed a number of steps in creating this resource:

1. We located citations to sources that we believed would contain useful information and ideas on doing case study research (e.g., general books about doing research, books about qualitative research and case studies).
2. We reviewed each of the books to identify those that provided us with an opportunity to illustrate a variety of perspectives about doing case study research.
3. We prepared a citation for each book and wrote an annotation that reflected the central theme and scope of the book as well as how it added developing knowledge about doing case study research.

Bassey, M. (1999). *Case study research in educational settings*. Philadelphia: Open University Press.

The aim of this book is to reconstruct the concept of educational case study as a prime strategy for developing educational theory that illuminates educational policy and enhances educational practice. It is offered to all who set out to conduct educational research by case study. It gives new insight into case study as a tool of educational research. Several different kinds of educational case study are identified: theory-seeking, theory-testing, storytelling, picture-drawing, and evaluative case study. A unique feature of the text is the author's advocacy of "fuzzy-generalizations"; it is argued that, in any case, qualitative fuzzy-generalizations are more honest and more appropriate in much research in educational settings than are definitive claims for generalizability because of the complexity that is usually involved. This text makes extensive use of examples of research projects that illustrate the various forms of potential of the approach as well as demonstrating the practicalities involved in setting up and executing case study work.

Berg, B. L. (2004). *Qualitative research methods for the social sciences* (5th ed.). New York: Pearson Education.

This text serves as a handbook for anyone interested in but unfamiliar with qualitative research methods. The central purpose of the book is to instruct inexperienced researchers in ways of effectively collecting, organizing, and making sense of qualitative information. It also seeks to demystify the research process. Novice researchers will learn how the process works, thus becoming comfortable and relaxed. Readers are moved beyond the point of collecting information without knowing what to do with it. In essence, the goal is to get fledgling researchers to design, collect, and analyze information, then present their results to the scientific community. It also incorporates discussion of Web sites, and their locations on the Web, as useful pieces of literature and qualitative research tools. In addition, seasoned researchers will find interesting opinions and discussions of topics that may expand their viewpoints beyond traditional perspectives.

Bogden, R. C., & Bilken, S. K. (2003). *Qualitative research in education: An introduction to theories and methods* (4th ed.). New York: Allyn and Bacon.

The purpose of this text is to provide a background for understanding the uses of qualitative research in education, to examine its theoretical and historical underpinnings, and to discuss specific methods for conducting research. It is primarily useful to those just beginning; however, it is also a valuable handbook for those practicing research. This book is organized in a manner that parallels the process of doing research; therefore, as students read about a particular phase of qualitative research they can be engaged in those activities.

Creswell, J. W. (1998). *Qualitative inquiry and research design: Choosing among five traditions.* Thousand Oaks, CA: Sage.

The basic premise of this book is that different forms of qualitative traditions exist and that the design of research within each has distinctive features. This book attempts to answer the question, How does the type or tradition of qualitative inquiry shape the design of a study? The uniqueness of this text is found in examining the reasons for the book. First, those conducting qualitative research do not always understand the tradition they are using and its chief elements. Second, those conducting qualitative studies need to consider the differences between approaches to qualitative research. Third, no book currently addresses the relationship of tradition and research design. Finally, for individuals trained or socialized in a specific tradition, this comparative analysis can enlarge their scope of inquiry methods and encourage them to seek out alternative procedures. The level of discussion involved in this text is suitable for upper-division and graduate students.

Creswell, J. W. (2005). *Educational research: Planning, conducting, and evaluating quantitative and qualitative research* (2nd ed.). Upper Saddle River, NJ: Pearson Merrill Prentice Hall.

The philosophy that guides the development of this text is twofold. First, research involves a process of activities rather than the application of isolated, unrelated concepts and ideas. Second, the educational researcher today needs a large toolbox of approaches to study the complex educational issues in our society. This text is the first introduction to educational research to offer a truly balanced, inclusive, and integrated overview of the field as it currently stands. The book's coverage is unique in its balanced presentation of quantitative, qualitative, and mixed-method research. Moreover, it consistently examines foundational issues of research from both quantitative and qualitative perspectives. This approach helps students understand fundamental differences and similarities between these approaches.

Denzin, N. K., Lincoln, Y. S. (Eds.). (2003). *The landscape of qualitative research: Theories and issues.* Thousand Oaks, CA: Sage.

This text is part of a three-volume student/classroom version of the *Handbook of Qualitative Research*. It should serve as a starting point, a springboard for new thought and new work. This book looks at the field from a broad theoretical perspective. It aims to give a wide orientation to the breadth and nature of the methods deemed to lie within the qualitative paradigm, giving an overview of the history, diversity, and future of the methods through detailed discussion and comparison of them. It is not a how-to book of the procedures and methods. There was consensus that this reorganization made a great deal of sense both pedagogically and economically. There is a definite commitment to make this iteration of the *Handbook* accessible for classroom use; this is reflected in the size, organization, and price of the paperbacks, as well as the addition of end-of-book bibliographies.

Gillham, B. (2002). *Case study research methods*. New York: Continuum.

This series is intended for those doing small-scale research in real-life settings. No previous knowledge of research methods is assumed. The thinking underlying the series reflects a major shift in social science research methods over the past 15 years—away from a natural-sciences style that emphasizes deductive theory-testing toward a recognition that such requirements are often unworkable and inappropriate in the real world. Readers are encouraged to not give up an empirical, evidence-based research tradition, but rather adapt to what is possible and, more important, what is likely to yield a truer picture.

Lyne, L. S. (2003). *A cross section of educational research: Journal articles for discussion and evaluation* (2nd ed.). Los Angeles: Pyrczak.

This text is designed for students who are learning how to evaluate published educational research. It contains 30 articles drawn from 21 different journals. The articles illustrate straightforward designs and the use of basic statistics. Each article deals with topics of interest to classroom teachers. In addition, the articles illustrate a wide variety of approaches to research. The articles were drawn from a large number of different journals, thus allowing students to get a taste of the wide variations in educational research. Furthermore, to initiate student discussion, there are three types of questions at the end of each article: factual questions, questions for discussion, and questions about quality ratings.

Maxwell, J. A. (1996). *Qualitative research design: An interactive approach*. Thousand Oaks, CA: Sage.

This book is intended to provide advice on designing a qualitative study. It presents an approach to qualitative research that both captures what qualitative researchers really do and provides support and guidance for those embarking for the first time on designing a qualitative study. It renders advice on every part of the design process: figuring out what your study should accomplish, constructing a theoretical framework, developing research questions, deciding on strategies and methods for information collection and analysis, and planning how to deal with potential validity threats to your conclusions. Because the design is the logic and coherence of the research study, the focus is primarily on research design, rather than on proposal writing. The text incorporates a hands-on approach; thus, in order for the book to be most useful, one should have a qualitative research project in mind.

Merriam, S. B. (1998). *Qualitative research and case study applications in education.* San Francisco: Jossey-Bass.

The combination of a primary emphasis on qualitative research with applications to case study makes this book unique in the burgeoning literature of qualitative research. This book can be used by those who are interested only in qualitative research in general, or it can be consulted for assistance in conducting a case study in particular. Another defining characteristic of this book is its how-to, practical focus; the mechanics of conducting a qualitative study are presented in a simple, straightforward manner. Designing a qualitative study, collecting and analyzing information, and writing research reports are some of the book's topics that are logically presented and liberally illustrated to assist the researcher who desires some guidance in the process. The intended audience for this book, then, is teachers, researchers, and graduate students in education who are interested in understanding qualitative research and perhaps in conducting a qualitative case study.

Seidman, I. (2006). *Interviewing as a qualitative research: A guide for researchers in education and the social sciences* (3rd ed.). New York: Teachers College Press.

Interviews are a hallmark of many types of case studies. This text provides step-by-step guidance to the individual researcher about in-depth interviewing as a research methodology while at the same time connecting method and technique to the broader issues in qualitative research. The text centers on a phenomenological approach to in-depth interviewing; how to carry out this approach and the principles of adapting it to one's own goals are discussed. The discussions on interviewing across racial and ethnic groups has been extended, and a new section on interviewing "elites" and participants for whom English is not the first language has been added. Throughout the text readers are led to other, useful, related texts that could be important to them in developing their own research. In addition, the author introduces readers to the strengths and weaknesses of specific computer programs and the advantages and disadvantages of using them to analyze qualitative research information.

Stake, R. E. (1995). *The art of case study research.* Thousand Oaks, CA: Sage.

The purpose of this short, readable volume is to present a disciplined, qualitative mode of inquiry into a single case. A view of case studies is developed that draws from naturalistic, holistic, ethnographical, phenomenological, and biographical research methods. Guidance is provided on all aspects of qualitative single case study research, including developing research questions, gathering information, analyzing and interpreting information, the roles of the researcher, triangulation, and report writing. Explanations are accompanied by concrete examples, including the full text of a report from an evaluation Stake conducted of an elementary school in Chicago that was involved in school reform. The uniqueness of this text revolves around its centeredness as an introduction to a specialized type of case study research.

Travers, M. (2001). *Qualitative research through case studies.* Thousand Oaks, CA: Sage.

The author contends that few methods texts explain the distinction between method and methodology and that to achieve a higher standard in research projects and dissertations one must think and write about methodological issues. Real competence in qualitative research methods is acquired through understanding the methodological basis of classic studies and emulating the things you like about them in your own work. Therefore, the text is organized around summaries of a number of well-known or exemplary studies. Another unusual feature of this text is that it introduces different ways of conducting qualitative research through reviewing a number of different research traditions. The main objective of the text is to introduce communities of researchers and enable the reader to appreciate their objectives and how they write about the social world.

Yin, R. K. (2003). *Applications of case study research* (2nd ed.). Thousand Oaks, CA: Sage.

This book presents numerous completed case studies on a broad variety of topics. It is intended to provide additional information to improve the craft as well as provide specific, concrete examples to illustrate the importance of doing case studies. The selected case studies all put into practice sound principles of case study research, reflecting the entire range of processes and procedures from research design to research reporting. These case studies applications therefore identify and suggest solutions to problems commonly encountered when one is doing case studies. This text enables seasoned investigators and students alike to emulate case study research techniques and principles in their own research.

Yin, R. K. (2003). *Case study research: Designs and methods* (3rd ed.). Thousand Oaks, CA: Sage.

The objective of this book is to guide investigators and students who are trying to do case studies as a rigorous method of research. The book is distinctive in several ways. First, it is a comprehensive presentation of the case study method. Second, it gives detailed attention to case study designs and analysis, as compared to the traditional topic of case study information collection. The first two topics have received too little attention in existing texts, yet they create the greatest problems for those doing case studies. Third, the book makes reference to case studies in many different fields, illustrating points made in the text.

Index

About the Authors

Dawson R. Hancock currently serves as Chair of the Department of Educational Leadership at the University of North Carolina at Charlotte, where he teaches graduate courses in research, evaluation, and assessment. He has broad program-evaluation experience in local school districts and has conducted extensive research on teacher education and evaluation processes and on factors that influence student motivation to learn. His publications have appeared frequently in the *Journal of Educational Research, Assessment and Evaluation in Higher Education, Journal of Research and Development in Education, Assessment in Education: Principles, Policy, and Practice, Educational Forum, Educational Technology Research and Development, Journal of Research in Childhood Education, NASSP Bulletin*, and *Journal of General Education*.

Bob Algozzine currently teaches in the Department of Educational Leadership of the College of Education at the University of North Carolina at Charlotte. He has been a special education classroom teacher and college professor for more than 30 years in public schools and universities in New York, Virginia, Pennsylvania, Florida, and North Carolina and he is currently the Codirector of the Behavior and Reading Improvement Center at the University of North Carolina at Charlotte. Textbooks he has written are used in teacher preparation courses around the country. He has been a featured speaker at local, state, national, and international professional conferences and is widely recognized as an expert on effective teaching and special education research.